COMMERCIAL LEASES

MALCOLM BRAHAMS
MA (Oxon), Solicitor

with

NORMAN HARKER
FRICS, ACIArb

COLLINS
8 Grafton Street, London W1

Collins Professional and Technical Books
William Collins Sons & Co. Ltd
8 Grafton Street, London W1X 3LA

First published in Great Britain by
Collins Professional and Technical Books 1985

Distributed in the United States of America
by Sheridan House, Inc.

British Library Cataloguing in Publication Data

Brahams, Malcolm
    Commercial leases.
    1. Commercial leases——England
    I. Title   II. Harker, Norman
    344.2064′3462   KD905

ISBN 0–00–383044–6

Typeset by Cambrian Typesetters,
Frimley, Camberley, Surrey
Printed and bound in Great Britain by
Mackays of Chatham, Kent

Contents

To my dear wife, Diana, without whose encouragement
this book would never have been written.

Introduction

In our high streets, market places, precincts and industrial estates a commodity is regularly traded, but it is one which the casual passer-by might well fail to recognise – it is the buildings which make up these complexes; the shops, offices, warehouses and factories and the land on which they stand.

The trend in residential property in the United Kingdom has for many years been towards the freehold ownership of homes or, failing that, the purchase of a long lease. In the commercial sector, owner occupation is the exception rather than the rule. Businessmen feel that their capital can be more usefully employed in financing stock or the expansion of their enterprises, rather than 'tied up' in property. Frequently, even where a businessman or his company has started off as the owner of the freehold, the property is sold off and leased back to him.

In any event, the clear pattern in the sphere of business property is that on the one hand a group of property owners (who may be private investors, institutions such as pension funds or local authorities) own the buildings, while a separate group (shopkeepers, professional men, industrial concerns) hold leases which allow them to carry on their businesses in these buildings.

The leases that regulate the relationship between these two groups of people have generally been negotiated at arm's length and with the benefit of professional advice. The state has not intervened in this process to any significant extent. The major piece of legislation affecting business leases is Part II of the Landlord and Tenant Act 1954. Within this framework the parties have been left to strike their bargain in the context of whatever market forces apply to their particular circumstances.

Nevertheless, within the framework of the Landlord and Tenant Act and the play of market forces there has grown up a body of case law whose significance to the landlord or the tenant can be profound. If the parties are to have anything like equality of bargaining power, both they and their advisers need to be familiar with the legal framework and also the prevailing practice of those specialising in the field.

In my view, there is no need for anyone involved in commercial property to be at a disadvantage or to feel that there is some impenetrable mystique to the subject. The intention of this book is to guide anyone who is not an expert on the subject stage by stage through the process involved in the negotiation, completion, renewal and termination of a commercial lease, pointing out the main concepts to be grasped and pitfalls to be avoided along the way. The law stated in this work is as at 1st January 1985.

Malcolm Brahams
22 Buckingham Street
London W.C.2

Chapter 1

Property to let

The first step in the process of letting commercial property will be its placing on the market by the landlord. Almost always, for sound commercial reasons, he will retain an estate agent to do this for him. Even if the landlord is competent in such matters as advertising and the preparation of particulars, he will normally need advice about the rental to quote and will expect the agent to earn his commission by ensuring that the property is offered and ultimately let at the best rent obtainable. What are the legal factors the landlord and his agents must bear in mind at this initial stage?

Making the most of the premises

Even before he offers the property on the open market, the landlord should ask his surveyors or estate agents if there are steps he should take at this stage to enhance the marketability of the property. For instance:

(a) Are there works of a minor nature, such as painting the common parts, or even major works of refurbishment which would increase the rental value and make the property more attractive to potential tenants?
(b) Is the planning use or the use permitted by the head lease too restrictive at present? Would it be sensible to apply for planning consent or to seek the superior landlord's agreement to different or additional uses?

After resolving these preliminary points, the landlord should consider if it would be worthwhile offering the property to neighbouring owners or to his superior landlord before he places it on the open market.

As to the proper rental to quote in the agent's literature, the agent will sometimes propose a highly competitive rent to stimulate interest. This may be advisable in some market conditions, provided the landlord forms a clear idea of the rental he actually hopes to secure when terms are ultimately agreed.

Length of term

The question of what rent to charge and the frequency of rent reviews will be a matter for the agent's judgment of the market but the landlord will have to give some thought at the outset to the length of the term. He should be aware of the general right conferred by the Landlord and Tenant Act 1954 enabling tenants to renew their leases (except in specified circumstances: see Chapter 11) at a market rent fixed, if necessary, by the court.

Unless he can foresee a need to recover possession of the premises after a specified period, there seems no particular incentive for a landlord to create a short lease. Where circumstances permit, terms of between fifteen and twenty years with reviews every four or five years are common. If trading conditions are poor, it is likely that some resistance will be met from tenants fearful of entering into very long term commitments and here, again, the agent should be able to advise in the individual circumstances.

In particular, tenants are likely to be wary of taking a long lease where the property is an elderly one approaching the end of its useful life. Maintenance costs in such a building are likely to be high and the wise tenant will want to minimise his exposure to a full repairing covenant. The tenant should also remember that he is the one who will have to pay stamp duty once the lease is completed and that rates of stamp duty increase if the term is for more than seven years and increase again at thirty-five years. Also, leases for more than twenty-one years may require registration at the Land Registry.

Liability of original tenant

In considering the length of the lease it is vital that the tenant should appreciate that, as the original lessee, he will remain liable to the landlord even after the lease has been assigned to a third party. This is the doctrine called 'privity of contract'. A tenant can protect himself from its worst consequences by:

(a) taking a lease for a term no longer than he needs;
(b) ensuring that the lease gives him the right to sublet in such a way that he will retain some control over the actions of a subsequent occupier; and
(c) trying to negotiate that it will be a term of the lease that the landlord will accept a surrender at the tenant's option. This could be acceptable to the landlord where there is a new tenant available willing to take up a new lease on improved terms at the time of surrender.

Excluding the 1954 Act

Since 1969 it has, as the result of amendments introduced by the Law of Property Act of that year, been possible for the parties to opt out of sections 24 to 28 of the Landlord and Tenant Act 1954. These are the clauses which give business tenants the right to renew their leases. The requirements of the 1969 amendments (which are embodied in section 38(4) of the 1954 Act) are that the parties must apply jointly to the court for the tenant's rights to be excluded. The procedure is purely an administrative one. There is no hearing in open court. Usually the application will explain the landlord's motives: for instance, that the property is temporarily surplus to his requirements. The precise wording that will satisfy the court varies from one district to another but essentially the court's approval may be treated as a foregone conclusion. If it is the express desire of the parties to proceed in this way, the court will not usually interfere.

If the landlord does intend to limit the tenant's rights in this way, it is sensible to announce the fact in the agent's particulars. The procedure is still not widely employed (although in some parts of London it is gradually becoming more common) and will be likely to deter tenants where there are alternative premises available which carry the protection of the Act. In short, the landlord should have some compelling reason for deciding to exclude the renewal provisions of the Act (such as an early need to reoccupy the premises himself). He should be prepared to encounter some sales resistance and may have to concede a lower rental.

Planning use

The next factor to be considered is whether the premises have an authorised use under the Town and Country Planning Acts for the use for which they are to be let. It is no good advertising premises as 'Offices to Let' when their permitted use is that of a showroom. In some localities (and the agent should know this) it may be fairly easy to obtain planning consent for the desired use and the process of doing so not too prolonged. In such a case the agent should advise his client to apply for consent at once. In other localities, such as central London at the present time, there may be a general policy of resisting changes to office use. The landlord and his advisers should be realistic enough in such circumstances not to waste their time advertising 'offices' which may not be used as such, only to find that the potential tenant withdraws when his searches and enquiries reveal the true position. The tenant with special needs, however, may succeed in securing a consent which would not be generally available.

There is, of course, much covert use of residential 'suites' as offices, particularly in parts of central London. Likewise, there may be some areas where the local planning authority is desperately trying to encourage employment and is resisting the use of factory space for uses such as warehousing which do not have much labour content. It is naturally tempting for a landlord with empty space on his hands to try to let industrial premises off for warehousing or showroom use, but those indulging in such practices should bear in mind that however long an unauthorised use is carried on it will never become lawful (section 87 of the Town and Country Planning Act 1971). Moreover, failure to comply with an enforcement notice or stop notice served by the planning authority is a criminal offence and the offender can be liable to pay a substantial fine which increases for each day the breach continues. The least one can say is that landlords (or tenants) feeling desperate enough to break the planning laws should do so with their eyes open.

There is, however, a fairly common case in which an unwary landlord might innocently create a letting where the use appeared to be in order but which would fall foul of the Town and Country Planning Acts. This is where part of a property had, for example, been used as offices but this use was only ancillary to the principle use of the building, e.g. the owner of a retail shop might have wished to let off surplus office space above the shop. He should bear in mind that the offices, even if used as such by him, do not have an independent planning use as such but are merely ancillary to his retail business. The same would apply to an office block forming part of a factory complex or workshops attached to a retail shop. In each case, the unit which was to be detached from the remainder would have to be the subject of a planning application.

Restrictive covenants in freehold or superior title

The landlord, particularly if he is letting these particular premises for the first time, should ask his solicitor to check the deeds to establish whether there is some restriction on the title which might limit the type of trade the tenant is allowed to carry on. If his property is mortgaged, the letting will almost certainly require his lender's consent so the lender's attitude to his proposals should be investigated.

If there are restrictions of some kind on the title, the landlord and his advisers will have to try and assess whether they are of practical significance in relation to the proposed letting. Sometimes the restrictions are of such antiquity that they are either irrelevant (for instance covenants prohibiting soap boilers or tallow chandlers) or there is no one around interested in enforcing them. On the other hand, the covenant may be quite recent and actively enforced.

For example, a brewery which has too many public houses in a particular town might sell off its freehold interest in a former pub but impose restrictions on the title prohibiting the sale of alcohol in order to protect the trade of their remaining pubs in the area. If the landlord and his agents overlook this factor, they could waste valuable weeks trying to let the premises to, say, a restaurant that wanted to serve drinks or a supermarket whose management might withdraw on discovering they could not run an off licence department.

Restrictions in headlease

Where the landlord is not the freeholder but is himself the tenant of the premises in question under an existing lease (the 'headlease') he is likely to be aware that he holds the premises subject to numerous restrictions. Again, it makes good economic sense to anticipate any possible problems by getting hold of the headlease and providing the agent with a copy.

Almost all leases will require the superior landlord's consent to the proposed subletting but the landlord should also check whether he will be allowed to sublet part of his property (if this is what he is proposing to do), whether the provision of directors' guarantees is mandatory where the subtenant is to be a limited company, and the nature of any restrictions on the permitted use. All these factors will affect the way the property is marketed.

The landlord and his advisers must ask themselves whether the restrictions on subletting or changes of use are such that the superior landlord must be reasonable when approached for consent, or if the restrictions are absolute ones. They will also be alerted to the need to take up adequate references in good time, not only for the tenant (whose references the landlord will want to see anyway) but also for any guarantors the headlease may require.

Rent reviews in headlease

Another vital reason why the headlease must be consulted before preparing the agent's particulars involves the timing of the rent reviews. Many people will feel that the best arrangement is for the reviews in the sublease to be identical to those in the headlease or geared to them in some way. This ensures that the holder of the headlease (sometimes called the 'mesne landlord') does not suffer periods in which he has to pay more rent to the freeholder than he is able to collect from the subtenant, though it may also result in there being no profit rental after the first rent review. Sometimes the headlease will have, say, seven yearly reviews and the landlord will be able to secure more frequent reviews from the subtenant. Suffice it to say that the landlord and his agents must take the review arrangements and other major features of the headlease into consideration when offering the property to let.

Repairing liabilities

Landlords invariably aim to let their properties on 'Full Repairing and Insuring' terms so as to pass on to their tenants full and comprehensive liability for the care of the building. If it is initially in poor repair, the landlord will normally try and impose 'FR&I' terms even if he has to offer an initial rent free period to compensate the tenant for the costs he will incur in putting the premises straight.

Before taking on any repairing liability the tenant will need to seek advice from both his solicitor and his surveyor. The solicitor will explain the extent of the obligations the landlord seeks to impose and the surveyor should be able to advise on the likely cost to the tenant of rectifying any existing defects.

It must be stressed that a tenant who accepts a 'modern' full repairing covenant is assuming responsibility for 'putting' the property into good repair (*Proudfoot* v. *Hart* (1890)). The tenant's obligations do not extend to 'renewal' where it is substantially the whole of the premises that requires reconstruction (*Lurcott* v. *Wakely and Wheeler* (1911)) but a degree of renewal is implied by the usual covenant. Few purchasers of a freehold interest would dream of purchasing without a structural survey but many tenants do take FR&I leases without this elementary precaution. A competent survey can be a useful bargaining tool when the level of rent and the length of the rent free period is negotiated.

Letting part of a building

Special problems, which should be considered at this early stage, arise when only part of a building is being let. The matter of whether a superior lease allows this has been mentioned above. What must be determined in all cases is the nature of the landlord's and tenant's respective repairing obligations where the lease is only going to comprise a portion of the building.

Originally FR&I leases were only granted in respect of whole buildings but it is now increasingly common for landlords to aim to achieve substantially the same result (a 'clear lease') when a building is being let off in parts. In the very simplest case this may be possible merely by imposing full repairing obligations on each tenant in respect of the portion of the building he occupies. For instance, a building may consist of a lock-up shop unit with offices above which are reached by a separate street door and staircase. The landlord could aim at granting two separate FR&I leases, leaving the shop tenant responsible for repairing and decorating the lower part of the building (including the foundations) and the office tenant liable for the upper part (including the roof). Some minimal clauses would be needed to cover such matters as shared access to water tanks or dustbins areas but, so far as the offer to let and the agent's particulars are concerned, each portion of the premises can be offered on a full repairing lease and there will be no problems in implementing this.

Service charges help landlords achieve 'clear leases'

In the old days, more complex buildings such as office blocks or workshop buildings let to a multiplicity of tenants were let on the basis that the tenant was responsible for internal repairs and decorations only, leaving the landlord to carry out structural repairs, external decorations and maintenance of the common parts, lifts, heating, any caretaking or refuse disposal facilities and so forth. Nowadays, as was illustrated in the celebrated House of Lords case *O'May* v. *City of London Real Property Company* (1982), it is the ambition of most landlords to achieve 'clear leases' of buildings of this kind. Although the landlord will apparently have repairing obligations in such cases, by introducing a comprehensive service charge scheme he ensures that the cost of carrying them out will ultimately fall on the tenants. The value to the landlord of achieving such an arrangement is underlined by the evidence quoted by Lord Hailsham in the O'May case, that creation of a clear lease of offices in a city office block 'would be to enhance the value of the landlord's reversion by a sum somewhere between £1m and £2m and at the same time to render it more marketable'.

The landlord must therefore decide at the outset, before placing a portion of a building on the market, whether to create a comprehensive service charge scheme passing on all the normal landlord's obligations to the tenants. He may need guidance from the agents if this is a practical proposition. For instance, if the building or its installations are in poor or only moderate repair there could be resistance from tenants to the idea of taking on a share of the landlord's burdens which they might feel, with some justification, to be self-inflicted. In some areas it may not be the state of the building but the state of the market which affects his decision. This may be so depressed that there is no prospect of disposing of the premises on a 'clear lease' and, indeed, the landlord may be forced to grant a 'tenant's lease' in order to get the place off his hands.

Surveying the whole building

A tenant about to commit himself to a lease with a service charge will have to ask his surveyor to report on the state of repair not just of his own unit but of the entire building. Some service charge schemes expect the tenant to contribute to the cost not merely of repairing but also of *replacing* the lift, central heating, foundations and other costly items.

Legal costs

Finally, the desire of the landlord to have his solicitors paid by the incoming tenant should be clearly stated. There is a piece of legislation on the subject: the Costs of Leases Act 1958. It states:

'Notwithstanding any custom to the contrary, a party to a lease shall, unless the parties thereto agree otherwise in writing, be under no obligation to pay the whole or any part of any other party's solicitor's costs of the lease.'

In the writer's experience, the Act is, in practice, largely irrelevant. The occasions where the parties decide to enter into a written agreement before signing the lease itself are fairly limited. It will happen, for instance, where repairs are needed or a landlord's licence or planning consent is necessary before the lease can be formally completed. However, the usual pattern is that all the negotiations between the parties are intentionally made 'subject to contract' until the lease itself is exchanged and completed. As a result there is no 'agreement' to which the Cost of Leases Act can apply.

Nevertheless, unless payment of the landlord's costs is spelled out in the agent's particulars the tenant's solicitors may well strike out a provision to that effect in the draft lease on the grounds that it was 'not agreed in the course of negotiations'. Landlords often assume that the tenant must be responsible for their costs and of course, despite the 1958 Act, this has become the general rule; but in no sense is it a binding obligation on the prospective tenant. Like all other terms, it is a matter of what bargain has been struck by the parties.

Refunding additional and future expenses

If the landlord is hoping to recover more than just his own solicitor's fees this should also be made clear. For instance, unless he has been alerted to this prospective liability at the outset the tenant may be entirely justified in resisting the landlord's requests to pay his costs for obtaining licence to sublet from a superior landlord or perhaps the costs of an application to the court to exclude the renewal provisions of the Landlord and Tenant Act. Looking even further ahead, the courts have held that when leases are eventually renewed under the Landlord and Tenant Act, even if the old lease states that the tenant is responsible for legal costs, the landlord can not expect his costs to be paid on the new lease unless the old one refers specifically to the costs of renewal (*Cairnplace Ltd* v. *CBI (Property Investment) Co. Ltd* (1984)).

Intelligent anticipation saves time

All these factors which I have urged the landlord and his agents to consider at the initial stage apply with equal force to the tenant and his advisers. The earlier in the process that both parties contemplate the legal as well as the commercial structure of their proposed tenancy, the more likely it is that the process can move to a conclusion satisfactory to both parties. The matters mentioned in this chapter are by no means exhaustive. Others which merit attention at the earliest stage of a commercial letting will appear in the course of subsequent chapters.

Even in their initial negotiations, the parties should certainly discuss the major terms of the lease. There can be substantial delays, indeed the letting may prove completely abortive, because the parties failed to reach agreement at the outset on the major clauses of importance to them. It is good negotiating practice and makes good commercial sense to agree any special clauses at this stage and not wait for the initial draft lease to arrive from the landlord's solicitors.

These observations are intended to encourage the parties and their advisers to approach their intended creation of a commercial lease with intelligent anticipation of the main pitfalls.

Chapter 2

It's a deal – subject to contract

Sooner or later, if the property has been successfully marketed, the landlord or his agent will be approached by a potential tenant ready to take the premises at a rent acceptable to the landlord. But property is not like stocks and shares. The deal is not concluded by a nod or the shaking of hands. There is still much negotiating of fine detail to be done. For this reason, even if both parties are satisfied with the basic terms they will normally go to some trouble to avoid being contractually bound at this early stage.

'Subject to contract'

This is generally achieved by putting words such as 'subject to contract' or 'contract denied' on any written record of the letting that has been negotiated and is effective because to be enforceable in the courts contracts relating to land must be evidenced in writing.

This requirement derives from one of the best known provisions in property law, namely section 40 of the Law of Property Act 1925 which states:

> 'No action may be brought on any contract for the sale or other disposition in land unless the agreement upon which such action is brought or some note or memorandum thereof is in writing and signed by the party to be charged or by some other person thereunto by him lawfully authorised.'

It should follow that any writing that bears suitable words negativing the existence of a contract can be disregarded. (In *Alpenstow Ltd and Another* v. *Regalian Properties Ltd* (1984) the words 'subject to contract' were disregarded by the High Court but this was an exceptional case where a detailed and conscientiously drawn document containing the words 'subject to contract' replaced a previously binding agreement.) However, if the parties act in such a way as to imply that a binding contract is in existence, then even a verbal contract to grant a lease or tenancy could be enforceable; for example, if the landlord accepts an advance payment of rent or allows the tenant into occupation to carry out repairs or improvements. In such cases, even if there is no writing, there may be enough evidence to support a claim that there is a verbal contract and the so-called 'Act of Part Performance' will allow the courts to uphold the tenancy.

Does payment make unwritten contract enforceable?

At one time it seemed to be settled law that payment of rent in advance was not of itself enough to allow an oral agreement for lease to be enforced (*Chaproniere* v. *Lambert* (1917)), but more recently, in the case of *Steadman* v. *Steadman* (1976), the House of Lords held that the payment of money alone might be sufficient. The circumstances were rather unusual as they related to a divorcing couple who made an oral agreement including the transfer of the matrimonial home. One party paid off some rent arrears and the court considered that this was 'a sufficient Act of Part Performance' to allow the enforcement of the contract to effect a transfer of the property. This underlines the need to record the fact that any money paid over as a deposit, reservation fee or advance payment of rent is 'subject to contract', unless of course the parties wish to be contractually bound at that stage.

There may be occasions where either the tenant or the landlord is so keen to conclude the deal that he will deliberately refrain from qualifying his correspondence in order to ensure that the landlord or tenant, as the case may be, is bound at the earliest moment. This may prove effective, but could rebound on the party seeking to benefit from the ploy because he may well have overlooked the inclusion of vital terms to protect his interest. For instance, an anxious landlord accepting his first quarter's rent from an eager tenant may not be able to point to any terms of the tenancy which would restrict the tenant's right to sublet – an omission he might later regret. Similarly, an eager tenant, on making his local searches and enquiries, may discover he is prohibited from carrying on his business at the property, or that there are road widening proposals which will disrupt his activities.

On balance, it does, therefore, seem to be in the overwhelming interests of both landlord and tenant to avoid a legal commitment until a proper lease or tenancy agreement has been drawn up and both parties have had the time to make their searches, inspections and enquiries, including references for the prospective tenant.

Written 'subject to contract' offer desirable

Having warned the tenant against committing himself in writing, I do not mean to say that he should not embody his proposal to take the tenancy in the form of a written offer. On the contrary, so long as it is 'subject to contract' it will be of great assistance in setting out the main matters that are of importance to him and can be used as the basis upon which the lease will be prepared.

As the landlord's agent has usually prepared printed particulars, the tenant or his agent should, in their offer, take care to spell out the ways in which their proposal differs from these. There may, for example, be certain terms of the tenancy as agreed verbally with the landlord's agent which diverge from the particulars. The particulars may specify three-yearly rent reviews but the tenant has agreed five; the agent may have conceded that the tenant does not have to pay the landlord's legal costs; the right to sublet particular portions of the property may have been mentioned and could be of importance if the letting is to be an economic proposition to the tenant. All these variations, whether already agreed on behalf of the landlord or additional matters which have occurred to the tenant, should ideally be incorporated in the 'subject to contract' offer. In this way later misunderstandings and disputes as to what was actually agreed can be avoided saving, in turn, both time and costs.

An example of the kind of letter the landlord's agent should write to the parties and their solicitors is set out in Appendix A. If it became universal practice to write letters of this kind in the field of commercial lettings, all the participants would stand to benefit. Abortive costs, delays, frustration and complaints can be minimised if an effort is made to agree the major terms of the transaction and to record them in this way before putting the matter in the hands of the parties' solicitors.

Outlining tenant's requirements

There will also be matters relating to the physical nature of the property. Will the tenant need to carry out alterations, repairs or improvements? Has the landlord agreed to carry out some initial repairs himself? Has he agreed to allow a rent free period at the outset of the lease to compensate the tenant for putting the place into good repair at his own expense? Will the tenant's obligation to do initial repairs be reflected in subsequent rent reviews? What about signs displaying the name and business of the tenant? Arc there shared loading facilities? What about fixtures? Are the agent's particulars sufficiently precise as to what is or is not included in the letting in the way of heating, lighting, carpets or other floor coverings, internal telephones, window blinds and the like? Again, a systematic appraisal of such matters and specific mention of them at this stage will smooth the way towards completion of the letting on agreed terms.

One reason why this initial correspondence is particularly useful is that in the majority of cases there will be no separate contract signed by the parties before completion itself takes place. This is in contrast to the almost universal convention adopted for sales and purchases of freehold land in England and Wales (or, for that matter, the disposal of existing leaseholds) where the transaction evolves through two distinct stages: the period up to the point that contracts are signed and exchanged, and the subsequent completion at which money changes hands and physical possession of the property is transferred. The normal procedure for a commercial lease is for the terms to be agreed 'subject to contract' and then the draft lease to be submitted and agreed with the parties still not contractually bound to one another, the legal relationship of landlord and tenant arising only when the lease itself is formally exchanged.

Need for a separate agreement for lease

The above arrangement is suitable in many instances, but there will be some cases where the parties will feel that a separate contract is desirable. A separate contract may be necessary if there is likely to be a time lag between the moment the initial deal is concluded and point at which the lease may actually be granted. The most important category is the building agreement.

There are frequent instances where works, falling short of major construction, have to be carried out either by the landlord or the tenant as a condition of the tenancy. Sometimes such obligations will be spelled out in the lease and carried out, say, in the first six months of the tenancy. In other cases, completion of the works may be a precondition of the grant of the lease and it is in those circumstances that a separate contract, or 'agreement for lease', will be essential. Obviously neither the landlord nor the tenant will be keen to carry out works 'on spec' without the other party being compelled to complete the lease as soon as the required conditions have been fulfilled. The conditions need not be restricted to structural works. It could be that planning consent or the consent of a mortgagee or superior landlord must be obtained before the tenancy can be lawfully granted. In all such cases the parties have to balance the advantages of retaining their freedom of action against the risk that, during the consent process or while the works are being carried out, the other party will lose interest and look elsewhere.

A good example of where an agreement for lease may be useful is where the tenant will require an official licence before carrying on his business. This includes not only the traditional areas of the public house and off licence but also supermarkets where alcohol may be sold and, since the Local Government (Miscellaneous Provisions) Act 1982, sex shops.

Will the agreement attract DLT?

Where there is to be an 'agreement for lease' before the grant of the lease itself, the parties must pay attention to the nature of the condition that is to be fulfilled before the lease can be granted. In the case of an agreement for lease signed before the commencement of building operations, the parties must consider the possible Development Land Tax implications. The landlord will need to take specialist advice, not only as to the amount of the tax but also regarding the date the liability is 'triggered'.

An agreement for lease constitutes a 'material interest' for DLT purposes and the grant of the agreement will be a 'part disposal', causing DLT considerations to arise. Where the landlord's specialist advisers are of the opinion that liability should not be triggered by signing an agreement for lease, it should be possible to achieve the same commercial result by alternative means; for instance a conditional contract or an option, neither of which will trigger the charge.

Timing

This leads us to consider the general question of timing. Even if there is no separate agreement laying down a completion date, an expression of the parties' intentions in this regard may be useful. A landlord letting vacant property will be interested in completing and, hence, receiving rent at the earliest opportunity. This may not suit the tenant who, whilst wishing to appear keen, will have his own arrangements to make. If possible, a target date acceptable to both should be set. Often this is so many weeks 'from the submission of the draft lease' which has the merit of keeping the landlord's solicitor on his toes. Sometimes the tenant will call upon the landlord to take the property off the market and the landlord may well make it clear that he expects the tenant to sign the lease by a particular date if he is to comply with this request.

Generally, at this initial stage, it will smooth the way towards a successful conclusion of the transaction if the parties have set out in their 'subject to contract' correspondence not only the terms of the letting itself but also any preconditions and the required timing.

Chapter 3

Solicitors are instructed

It must be a matter of profound relief to solicitors as a profession that no real inroads have been made into their role in the drafting of leases, particularly in the commercial field. The 'do your own conveyancing' brigade have not advanced on to this particular territory largely because the property owners who create leases and the businessmen who take them recognise that there are sound commercial reasons for employing the services of the legal profession in these circumstances.

Can one solicitor act for both sides?

A small businessman may, nevertheless, be deterred by the cost of employing a solicitor particularly since, as the tenant, he will generally be expected to pay both his own costs and those of the landlord. For this reason he will sometimes be tempted to enquire whether the landlord's solicitor can act for him as well. The Law Society (in the *Gazette* 1972, Vol. 69, p. 1117) has ruled that solicitors are not to act for both sides, either on the transfer of land or the grant of a lease, unless both are established clients of the firm *and* provided, also, that there is no conflict of interest.

So long as there is no conflict, there are some limited exceptions to the need for both parties to be established clients; for instance, in small communities where there is only one firm that may be conveniently instructed, or where both landlord and tenant are close relations (or associated companies), or where associated firms of solicitors or different branches of the same firm are instructed by each side. However, even in these limited circumstances or where the landlord and the tenant have, by coincidence, always used the same solicitor, it is in my view very easy for a situation of conflict to develop.

It seems to me that the very relationship of landlord and tenant is naturally one of some tension between the two sides. As we shall see, the whole business of negotiating, drafting and approving the lease is one of give and take, proposal and counter-proposal, advantage and concession. In those circumstances, a solicitor who finds himself acting for both sides would need to take exceptional care to ensure that both his clients fully understood the precise nature of the documents and the degree to which such documents tended to favour one side or the other.

Moreover, the friendliest of parties do break up; families have rows and linked companies may end their association. It is best to accept that leases are granted on an adversarial basis, even where the adversaries are friendly.

A partial solution in cases where the tenant is very keen to retain the services of a firm which also acts for the landlord is for a different partner to act for each party. This can work quite well, but both solicitors have to keep a weather eye open for the possibility of a real conflict arising, at which point they will have the invidious task of directing one of their clients across the street to seek independent advice. Also, if the firm is charging on a time basis, the cost saving advantage of using a single firm will be partially defeated as two men's time will be taken up, though there could still be some saving of time and certainly of postage.

Doing without a solicitor

Where the tenant is so short of funds that he simply can not afford his own solicitor, it does sometimes happen that he will act for himself and rely on the landlord's solicitor to guide him through the necessary procedures. In such cases the landlord's solicitor will often try to be helpful but will generally be at pains to point out that he is not purporting to advise the tenant. The latter may perhaps be able to show the draft lease to a friend with legal training who can help him on an informal basis. I think it is fair to say, though, that he is likely to emerge with a lease that is not angled as much in his favour as would be the case if he were separately represented. This is quite apart from such other considerations as the need for searches and enquiries.

It is said among lawyers that the man who acts for himself has a poor adviser and a fool for a client. You would, of course, expect a member of the legal profession to be biassed. But I have been solemnly assured by a commercial property surveyor that he and his professional colleagues, who are involved with such leases on a daily basis and whose knowledge of matters of this kind rivals that of many solicitors, would rarely if ever act for themselves in taking or granting a lease.

Independent advice for guarantor?

Finally, where the director of a company or some other person is acting as a surety or guarantor he normally obtains advice from the same solicitor as the landlord. This may be quite proper in the case of a small private company where the directors and shareholders are the same people. In other cases, however, a guarantor should seriously consider taking independent legal advice. His interests are not the same as those of the tenant and he will need to be advised on the extent of his personal liability which may extend far beyond his immediate contemplation. Guarantees should never be given lightly.

The letter of instructions

Assuming that the general rule applies and each party has instructed solicitors, how can the parties help their lawyers to help them to achieve a speedy and effective agreement?

Once the deal is concluded on a 'subject to contract' basis, it is usual for the landlord or his agent to write either to the tenant or his solicitors setting out the agreed terms. This letter should set out not only the basic terms, such as rent and the length of the lease, but also any other essential features of the transaction that have been expressly agreed during the negotiations or which the agent feels have been implied by the circumstances. In the first category would be such matters as rent review dates, permitted use, legal costs, repairing obligations and the like. In the second could be the question of timing, the possibility of the tenant providing guarantors (particularly if all references have yet to be taken up), rights of way, service contributions (which may have been mentioned generally but on which the lawyers will need specific instructions) and any other matter which could come up as the lease is negotiated. (See

Appendix A for a sample letter of instructions covering a wide range of points.)

The importance of the detailed letter of instructions covering all the major aspects of the agreement the parties reached subject to contract can not be overstressed. It is a waste of time and costs to refer a proposed letting to solicitors without first ensuring that a basis for agreement actually exists. All too frequently a letting falls through at a late stage over a point that should have been identified at the pre-instruction stage. Sometimes one party will secure a concession (for instance a reduced rent) which could have been avoided if the matter in contention had been discussed at the negotiation stage. Although agents sometimes express their envy of solicitors who are able to charge for abortive work, such costs are by no means the mainstay of most solicitors' practices.

Standard leases favour landlords

Most solicitors hold one or more standard forms of lease which they use for the letting of business property and as these are to be submitted on behalf of the landlord they will tend to have a definite bias in the landlord's favour. The landlord's agent should therefore bear the basic terms of a conventional Full Repairing and Insuring lease in mind when formulating his letter of instructions to the landlord's solicitors and direct their attention to those features which are to deviate from the norm. Thus the letter from the landlord's agent should not only represent instructions to his client's solicitor, but also define the transaction as he sees it and provide a frame of reference within which both firms of solicitors can work.

The tenant's response

It follows that if the landlord's agent has provided a comprehensive letter the tenant may not need to give his own solicitor such detailed instructions at the initial stage; but as soon as he sees the letter he should confirm its contents or point out any factors which the landlord's agent may have got wrong or forgotten. A case in point is the matter of legal costs, which was discussed earlier. It often happens that neither side has discussed this question, but the landlord's agent lists payment of his client's costs as a matter of course. Another matter that the landlord's agent sometimes conveniently forgets is any rent free period which may have been offered. The tenant should be shown a copy of the letter of instructions and point out to his solicitor any matter which requires correction.

It is a counsel of perfection to expect both parties to have thought of everything at the initial stage. In the tenant's case it is perhaps only when he has agreed the basic terms that he begins to consider the physical problems of getting the premises ready for occupation and actually moving in. With luck, his solicitor will prompt him for instructions on his requirements for signs, partitioning, alterations generally and the need for access, if required, at a date preceding formal grant of the lease.

Securing further concessions

The tenant may also, either by accident or design, have left to his solicitor the task of securing concessions for his benefit. Although it will often be essential for the solicitor to take instructions on details once the draft lease is in his hands, the tenant can usefully indicate his general stance at the initial stage. Whatever may have been discussed with the agents the tenants may, after closer inspection or after receiving his surveyor's report, feel that the condition of the building is not all that could be desired and that a concession should be sought from the landlord; for instance, the extension of the rent free period or its introduction where there was none before. Alternatively, the tenant may require initial repairs to be carried out at the landlord's expense. In serious cases, a schedule of condition limiting the tenant's repairing liability may be proposed. If it was not canvassed with the agents, the landlord is likely to regard this idea as an impudent one, but the tenant may succeed in cases where there is no substantial competition for the property.

Often the initial negotiations will be not only 'subject to contract' but also 'subject to survey'. Sometimes the tenant will delay having his survey until he is reasonably sure that the property is 'his' and will use the result of the survey as a lever to secure last minute concessions. It may therefore be in the landlord's interests to stipulate that 'subject to survey' does not mean the tenant is free to renegotiate the lease unless major defects are discovered and the cost of repair would exceed a certain figure.

Tenant's plans for the future

The tenant should also outline to his solicitor his future plans for the property, as far as they can be foreseen at this stage. If he will not require the whole property for his personal use (or that of his business), he should make it clear that he will require the right to underlet part of the property. The possibility of occupation by subsidiary or associated companies should also be mentioned if applicable.

A careful inspection of the property after agreement on the basic terms is a good idea for it is a facet of human nature that different points will occur to the potential tenant when he knows he is likely to be the occupier from those he noticed on his initial inspection. When presented with the prospect of actually trading from the property, his mind will be focussed more sharply on such matters as outstanding repairs, access, loading bays, refuse arrangements, type and location of power points, and such mundane but essential matters as toilet facilities.

So far as the landlord is concerned, I have assumed that his agent will have outlined the salient terms to his solicitor. He should then, of course, point out any refinements or discrepancies that may occur to him. As it will be difficult for his solicitor to retract a clause that has been included in the draft lease as originally submitted, he should also take care to point out any requirements that would deviate from the solicitor's standard lease. Is there a particular trade he is anxious to prohibit, perhaps because it may compete with his own business interests? Is the lease of such a short duration that he would like to see an absolute bar on assignment or subletting? If only part of a building is being let, have all necessary rights been reserved to allow other occupiers access or the landlord's own contractors rights to carry out maintenance?

Lease plans

If there are complications of this nature the agents will, it is to be hoped, have provided a suitable plan. A well drawn plan, like the picture in the apocryphal Chinese proverb, is worth a thousand words to the solicitor drafting the lease. It should clearly direct his mind to problems like access, rights of way, common and exclusive areas and so forth. It would be useful if the solicitor could inspect the property itself, but this is an ideal that is impractical in many cases and a surveyor's plan is almost always an adequate substitute.

Show the agents the draft lease

Sometimes the landlord's solicitor will submit the draft lease to his client's agents for their comments before he sends it to the tenant's solicitor for approval. This can cause delay in submission of the initial draft, but greater delays may arise if changes have to be made at a later date. The agent should be able to make a contribution to the following matters:

(a) confirmation that the draft lease reflects the terms as he negotiated them;
(b) comments on the rent review clause including the basis of valuation;
(c) comments on the day to day management of the building and the service charge scheme;
(d) observations on practical problems which might arise on assignments, subletting or changes of use; and
(e) confirmation that the plans and the description of the property are correct and that the solicitors have remembered to include the appropriate rights and reservations.

In short, and this is a theme which runs throughout this book, intelligent anticipation by the parties and the communication of their needs to their professional advisers are of enormous importance to the achievement of the completed letting on terms acceptable to all parties.

Chapter 4

Picking your way through the draft lease

With the assistance of a word processor (or, if he is not fortunate enough to own such a machine, a photocopier and a pair of scissors) the landlord's solicitor assembles his lease and submits it, in duplicate, to the tenant's solicitor – all thirty-five pages or so. Despite the length of the document and the sophistication of the process by which it has been produced, most leases are in the same essential format as those painstakingly scrawled in copperplate handwriting by industrious clerks when Victoria was Queen. They start by listing the parties ('of the first part' etc.), pausing perhaps for the 'recitals' (recording the fact that the parties have reached agreement) and then plunging into the traditional 'operative words': the 'demise of the land', the 'parcels' (the description of the land) the 'habendum' (the term) and 'redendum' (the rent). There follow an extensive list of tenant's covenants, a rather shorter list of landlord's covenants, a number of pages of provisos – and there you are.

The use of archaic language is often desirable because the words in question have been considered by the courts and their precise meaning construed by the judges. However, many solicitors are becoming aware of the need to use plainer English in order to enhance their clients' understanding of the documents they prepare.

There may be superficial differences of format. For instance, many of the essential details may be grouped together in a schedule on the front page. But when such innovations are tossed aside, it is surprising how far the modern lease still conforms to the traditional pattern except, of course, that it is much longer. This may be due to modern technology or merely to the fact that life in the modern world is more complex, but whatever the cause the length of modern leases has drawn adverse criticism, particularly from those acting for the tenant, and the demand that the essential terms be embodied in some generally adopted set of conditions, like the National Conditions of Sale in the case of contracts or 'Table A' in the case of companies.

General lease conditions?

Within legal offices this system exists, in embryo, in the form of standard draft leases (or perhaps an array of variations to one basic draft) which make up that firm's set of precedents on the subject. Nevertheless, the need to tailor each lease to a particular set of circumstances means that it would be difficult, if not impossible, to design a widely accepted set of conditions.

The Law Society and the Royal Institution of Chartered Surveyors have agreed a model form of rent review clause. They suggest that this clause, which has several variants, is not appropriate for all cases and should, in effect, be used as a draft. The two Societies are now working on a similar clause relating to service charges and, doubtless, the same recommendations will apply. As far as I am aware, however, there has to date been no effective move to promote a generally adopted set of conditions.

It is, perhaps, the sheer variety of buildings to which commercial leases have to adapt themselves which encourages lawyers to stick to their own forms of tailor made lease, coupled perhaps to the suspicion that a nationally promoted form might prove less favourable to the landlord.

Checklist

Be that as it may, the tenant's solicitor will be presented with a complex document of which he may show his client a copy or possibly a summary. For easy reference, and to help pick out the points likely to be of significance to his client, it is helpful to prepare a checklist or chart. An example of the checklist I have used for several years is shown in Appendix B. It is not exhaustive, and its completion is no substitute for careful perusal and amendment of the draft lease, but it does help pick out the main items of contention and allows particular points to be verified at a glance without the need to look through the entire document.

What should the tenant's solicitor, his surveyor and indeed the tenant himself look out for at this stage? First and foremost, has the draft prepared by the landlord's solicitor incorporated correctly the principle terms reached in the earlier negotiations? The solicitor has, we hope, got the term and the rent right but is the property correctly and clearly defined? Is any plan a correct representation of what is to be let?

Plans for identification only

There has recently been some withering judicial comment on the poor quality of the plans used by conveyancing solicitors. Of course, a plan is not always essential and if there is both a plan and a clear verbal description of the property it is the words that will take precedence.

Often the draft lease will say something like:

> all that piece of land known as 45 High Street Bromley together with the building erected thereon as the same is *for purposes of identification only* shown edged red on the plan annexed hereto.

It used to be thought that the phrase 'for identification only' meant that the plan could only be regarded as being for rough guidance, but the 1978 Court of Appeal case *Wigginton and Milner Ltd* v. *Winster Engineering Limited* clarified the position. It is still true that, where these words are used to describe the plan, clear wording will take precedence but if the verbal description is of a general nature the plan will be regarded as an accurate indication of what has been let.

It is surprising how often plans are incorrect or the area of the site or the building incorrectly quoted. At best the mistake will cause embarrassment, inconvenience and the cost of rectification or correction of the documents. At worst, another letting or a sale will encroach over the boundary or a new building may be erected before the mistake is realised.

Access rights

Where the tenant will need access over a driveway, a footpath or a rear passageway, the plan or verbal description of the property must make this clear. The lease must also specify whether the tenant will have the use of installations such as the lift (for passengers and/or goods), loading bays, parking facilities and so forth.

Leases always reserve rights in favour of a landlord who owns adjoining property to enter the tenant's land to enable him to repair his own neighbouring building. He may also have to reserve additional rights for himself and his other tenants. An example would be a right to cross the tenant's property to reach a fire escape.

Covenants against alterations, assigning and changes of use

The next consideration is the set of covenants against alterations, dealing with the property and changes of use. In each case the tenant will need to know if the prohibitions are absolute or merely qualified, i.e. permitted subject to the landlord's consent. If the latter, does the lease in each case state that consent is not to be unreasonably withheld? If not, it should be borne in mind that there are two major cases where reasonableness is implied by section 19 of the Landlord and Tenant Act 1927. Where the landlord's consent is required, it must not be unreasonably withheld to a request for assignment or subletting. The same applies to alterations, but only so long as they represent an improvement to the premises. It should be specially noted, however, that a covenant against the tenant changing the use of the property without the landlord's consent does *not* carry with it any implied obligation for the landlord to be reasonable. This can be a trap for the unwary.

For example, in the case of *Sykes* v. *Midland Bank Executor & Trustee Co.* (1971), where offices were restricted to use by architects and the tenants wanted to assign the lease to persons carrying on a different business, the restricted use operated, in practice, as a bar on assignment unless the tenants were fortunate enough to find another firm of architects to take over the premises. They were able to recover damages from their solicitor (in fact from his executors) for his failure to draw his clients' attention to the point. At the time I was practising from a different floor of the same building in Regent Street and my senior partner lost no time in sending round a tautly worded memo drawing our attention to the object lesson provided by that case which was literally so close to home.

A litigious field

The law governing consent for changes of use is currently regarded as a field for potential litigation, but the present position is as follows:

(a) If the covenant against changing the use of the property is absolute and unqualified, the landlord is able to impose any terms or demands he wishes in return for granting his consent.

(b) If the lease allows a change of use 'with the consent of the landlord', section 19 (3) of the Landlord and Tenant Act 1927 specifies that no fine or premium may be *demanded* for consent. However, the section does *not* imply that consent should not be unreasonably withheld and does not prevent a landlord from accepting a fine or premium. In *Guardian Assurance Company Ltd* v. *Gants Hill Holdings Ltd* (1983) it was argued that under the common law the court should imply that where the landlord's consent was required it should not be unreasonably withheld. This argument was rejected in the High Court, but the point may be raised in other cases in the Court of Appeal. The best way to avoid disputes during the course of the tenancy is for the parties to decide at the outset whether or not the restriction on use is to be an absolute one. If it is not, then the words 'not to be unreasonably withheld' should be written into the lease.

(c) Where the lease *does* specify that the landlord's consent is not to be unreasonably withheld, there are a number of decided cases which provide guidelines as to what is and is not unreasonable (see Chapter 7).

Opening up the user clause

The tenant's solicitor will normally be acting in his client's interests if he opens up the user clause, either to allow any change with consent which is not to be unreasonably withheld or, at least, to permit changes within a wide general category of business corresponding, perhaps, to the Town and Country Planning Use Classes Order.

    The universal adoption of rent review clauses has brought about a relaxation in the user clauses now found in many leases. This is not altruism on the landlord's part but the realisation that where the lease has an open user clause the level of rent on review will be greater than where the use is very restricted. There has therefore been a turn around in practice to some extent and indeed a tenant's solicitor who opens up a restrictive user clause must bear in mind that he will be paving the way to an enhanced rent for the landlord when the reviews arise. On balance, I am inclined to think that an open user clause is to the tenant's benefit, but there may be special cases where a specific and restricted user would be in the tenant's interest.

Rent review clauses

The subject of rent reviews deserves – and gets – a separate chapter to itself (Chapter 9). Nevertheless we must at this stage consider the major features of drafting that will be significant to the parties.

The landlord's interests will be served by ensuring that the rent review mechanism does not catch him out by prescribing time limits or procedures with which he may fail to comply. If the review clause is drafted to make 'time of the essence', then failure to comply with its strict requirements could result in the landlord losing the review or the tenant losing his right to negotiate the rent or to have the review referred to an independent surveyor.

Since the celebrated case of *United Scientific Holdings Ltd* v. *Burnley Borough Council* (1978) it is firmly established that time limits for the service of rent review notices (or referring the rent to arbitration) are not strict unless the lease spells out that 'time is to be of the essence'. But beware: this ruling does not apply to options or renewals or to the purchase of the freehold where time limits may be taken literally.

Break clause with review clause

Occasionally, to confuse the issue, a 'break clause' may be intertwined with the rent review clause. This happened in the case of *Al Saloom* v. *James (Shirley) Travel Service Ltd* (1981). The tenant had the right to terminate the lease on six months' notice at the end of the third year of the term. At the same time the landlord could give a rent review notice 'not more than twelve nor less than six months' prior to the expiration of the third year. The landlord served his notice on 5 January but the six-month period prescribed by the lease required him to do so by 24 December. The lease did not expressly make time of the essence but the Appeal Court decided that, because the review clause and the break clause were linked, the review notice was invalid.

In contrast, where there is a straightforward rent review clause and time is not of the essence, quite extravagant delays in serving trigger notices have been held not to invalidate the review (see *Amherst* v. *James Walker Goldsmith & Silversmith Ltd* (1983)).

It is a matter of preference, but my inclination is to dispense altogether with the need for a trigger notice and simply state that the rent will be reviewed on the specified dates with machinery to fix the rent if agreement is not reached. The RICS/Law Society model clause does not require a trigger notice. If the parties prefer to incorporate one, then it is advisable to spell out the fact that time is *not* to be regarded as being of the essence.

Can landlord dictate rent if tenant fails to respond?

So far as the tenant is concerned, he should be wary in particular of the type of notice that allows the landlord to impose the rent of his choice unless the tenant objects by serving a counter notice at a stated time. In such cases it is important to ensure that the counter notice is in the specified form. A simple objection by the tenant to the rent specified in a notice of this kind will not serve as a notice *electing* to have the rent referred to an expert or an arbitrator.

It may seem incredible, but numerous landlords have got away with the imposition of very advantageous rents in this way (*Sheridan* v. *Blaircourt Investments Ltd* (1984)). The tenant may be inexperienced or may simply have a blind spot so far as official-looking notices are concerned. Perhaps he hopes the rent review will go away. On the other hand, the tenant should try to avoid the possibility of the review process being over long. The landlord may well see advantages in delaying the review for some months so that more and later 'comparables' may be brought in as evidence. This means a prolonged period of uncertainty for the tenant with the prospect of a substantial bill for excess rent, sometimes with interest, once the review is finally concluded. His solicitor should therefore try to secure wording which will allow the tenant to bring the review to a head himself if the landlord is dragging his feet.

Review clause: does it assume too much?

The tenant and his advisers should also scrutinise the review clause to see what criteria are adopted for fixing the market rent. Will the new rent be fixed on unwarranted assumptions? In the case of *Pugh* v. *Smiths Industries Ltd* (1982), for example, the rent had to be determined as though the remainder of the lease were at a fixed rent, without reviews, for the remainder of the twenty-five year term. There were, in fact, reviews every five years, so the assumption was fictitious; but, nevertheless, the court could not upset the bargain struck by the parties and as a result the rent was fixed at £36,750 whereas if the existence of later reviews had been recognised it would have been £30,600.

It is quite usual for the landlord to concede that the review clause should ignore the same factors which the court is required to ignore in fixing the rent upon renewal of a lease under section 34 of the Landlord and Tenant Act. These are, briefly, the fact that the tenant is already occupying the property (so that he might pay more to avoid the nuisance of moving), the goodwill of his business and any improvements executed by the tenant during his occupancy. There really should be no difficulty in securing these concessions for the purpose of the rent reviews: they are well established for lease renewals and widely recognised as fair. However, the wording of section 34 may not fit every case and it should be adapted to suit the circumstances.

The object of fairness should be kept in mind by both parties. The tenant must be concerned to see that he is not wrong-footed into agreeing criteria which will give the landlord an unreasonable advantage. The landlord is entitled to ensure that the rent which is to be fixed will be equivalent to what he could expect to secure for the property on the open market at the time of each review.

Service charges

Where less than the whole building is being let, it is probable that a service charge will be required. As I observed in Chapter 1 the landlord will usually do his best to concoct a scheme that will allow him to recover a proportion of all his foreseeable expenses. The tenant, who will have had advance notice of the service charge arrangements in a general sort of way, should be made aware of the kind of commitment he is undertaking. Many will be willing to accept whatever the landlord proposes as a necessary evil and part of the price paid for admission to the premises.

There is, as yet, no equivalent for commercial property of the protection afforded to leaseholders of flats by Schedule 19 of the Housing Act 1980. The obligations of the parties are entirely governed by the terms of the lease and the general law of contract and it is therefore all the more important to scrutinise the lease carefully. The particular matters that need watching are:

(a) Is the advance estimate entirely at the discretion of the landlord or his surveyor?
(b) Is there any express term requiring the landlord to be reasonable over both what he spends and what he is entitled to collect in advance?
(c) Is the landlord obliged to get the accounts audited by a properly qualified person?
(d) Will the landlord be able to undertake capital projects, such as replacing the lift or repointing the brickwork, at the tenant's expense? In the case of short leases this should certainly be resisted. In the case of longer leases the tenant should not be trapped into having to contribute to the capital costs and then, on review, to pay a rent that reflects the very improvements for which he has paid.
(e) Is the proportion payable correctly and fairly calculated?
(f) Is the landlord seeking to recover his own or an 'in house' agent's management fees?
(g) How will VAT returns be affected?
(h) Will the service charge in the initial years reflect existing defects in the building?
(i) Is there a sinking fund to cover major capital expenditure?
(j) Are other tenants in the building participating in the scheme and paying their due contributions? Will the landlord contribute his share if he occupies part of the building himself or if there is a void?
(k) How does the service charge clause match up with the landlord's repairing obligations?

Landlord's covenants

Conventionally, after a very long list of tenant's obligations the number of landlord's covenants will seem meagre by comparison. The landlord will offer the tenant 'quiet enjoyment' of the property which means, essentially, that 'the ordinary and lawful enjoyment of the demised land is not substantially interfered with by the landlord' (*Sanderson* v. *Berwick upon Tweed Corporation* 1884)).

Insurance

The landlord will normally covenant to effect insurance, although in most cases it is the tenant who will be paying the premium. The risks covered apart from fire will be mentioned. The landlord will not want to be tied down to insuring risks that may, in the future, prove uneconomic and general words like 'the normal comprehensive terms' or, more usually, 'such other risks as the landlord or its surveyor may deem expedient' will be found. The tenant and his advisers should attempt to get more specific wording introduced here – certainly explosion, riot and civil commotion. There will also be provision for insuring architects' and surveyors' fees (in connection with the works of reconstruction) and site clearance charges, and a covenant by the landlord to use the insurance monies paid over to him for the reconstruction of the building.

Landlords do not normally object to the tenant demanding more extensive cover where the tenant is paying the cost unless the cover is beyond the level being effected in the rest of the building. In such a case the tenant is at liberty to arrange his own 'top up' cover.

Loss of rent: Suspension of rent

A couple of clauses that must be read in conjunction relate to the situation that occurs when all or part of the property becomes unusable following a fire or as a result of one of the other risks against which insurance has been effected. First, as part of his insurance covenant the landlord will cover loss of rent so that his income from the property will continue notwithstanding the damage it has suffered. Secondly, there will be a 'proviso' that rent (or at least part of it) will be suspended after the building has been damaged until it is reinstated. The landlord will wish to avoid any discrepancy between the period insured, say two years, and the maximum period for which rent need not be paid. At the same time, the tenant may fairly point out that as it is the landlord who insures and has taken upon himself the obligation to rebuild, it is only right that the rent should remain suspended for an indefinite period, i.e. until the reinstatement is complete.

An impasse of this kind is frequently compromised by the parties agreeing to insure three years' loss of rent and extending the suspension period to the same term. An alternative which the landlord may wish to consider is a provision allowing the lease to be terminated if rebuilding is likely to be impracticable or, perhaps, if major damage would afford an opportunity of major reconstruction. The parties must then get over the question of whether the tenant, who in theory has no capital interest in the building, should receive any part of the insurance monies.

Inadequate cover

In *Beacon Carpets Ltd* v. *Kirby and Another* (1984) the Court of Appeal considered a situation where the premises had been underinsured. The cover was £30,000 whereas the cost of reinstatement was £50,000. After site clearance costs and some payment for loss of rent, the sum remaining was only just over £26,500 and this was placed on deposit while the parties litigated. Due to continuing delays, the tenant eventually decided to surrender his lease but persisted with his claim for damages against the landlord for underinsuring and for the delay. Both the High Court and the Court of Appeal awarded the tenant only £2 nominal damages but decided the insurance monies should belong to the landlord and the tenant in proportion to the respective interests of the parties. The appropriate date was the date of the fire as that was when the right to the policy monies arose.

This case illustrates two practical considerations. Tenants should consider what they might wish to do in the case of a major fire. Firstly, if they are likely to be kept out of occupation for a considerable time, should they be able to surrender? Conversely, should the landlord be permitted to require a surrender? Secondly, the tenant's right to compensation for the loss of his interest is usually totally inadequate to cover his losses and the tenant must ensure that either he or the landlord takes out cover for his consequential losses.

Extra covenants the tenant should call for

Beyond the basic landlord's covenants to grant quiet enjoyment and effect insurance, there are two major instances where the tenant is entitled to call for additional covenants even if none are volunteered. Where the landlord himself is a leaseholder, it is only reasonable that he should give the tenant a covenant to pay the ground rent under the headlease and to observe such of the headlease covenants as are not already the direct obligation of the tenant in the proposed underlease. Where a headlease is forfeited by the court, any subleases granted out of it are also forfeit. Although in these circumstances the subtenant has a good chance of persuading the court to grant relief from forfeiture of the underlease he holds, it is helpful if he reserves the right of redress by having taken a direct covenant of indemnity from the landlord. Of course, if the landlord's default has arisen because he is insolvent, the existence of an indemnity will be academic; but in all other cases it should be of some avail in minimising the tenant's exposure to the consequences of a breach of the headlease.

Title paramount

Another way the tenant's solicitor can seek to protect his client where there is a superior landlord is by trying to get the usual form of covenant for quiet enjoyment extended so as to make it clear that the landlord is also offering an undertaking that the tenant's occupation will not be interrupted by 'persons claiming by title paramount'. Without these words, the tenant may be deprived of the chance of a direct claim against his immediate landlord in circumstances where the immediate landlord is in arrears with his rent under the headlease and the subtenant is, in consequence, evicted (*Kelly* v. *Rogers* (1892)).

Can the landlord be obliged to do repairs?

A further case where the tenant should look to the landlord to undertake additional obligations is where the lease does not place direct and comprehensive repairing obligations on the tenant. On the one hand, this can occur where the lease is on internal repairing terms only (perhaps because the building is in poor repair and can only be let upon such terms, or where part only of the building is being let); on the other hand, there are many occasions where the tenant is only indirectly responsible for exterior and structural repairs through the imposition of a service charge. In both cases it can frequently occur that the landlord or his solicitors will deliberately fail to insert positive covenants to repair by the landlord. The lease will restrict the tenant to repairing the interior and may require him to contribute to the cost of any exterior repairs (or repairs to common parts) the landlord may care to undertake, but will refrain from saying who is to carry out such repairs if they are required.

There is, at present, no equivalent provision for commercial property to the obligations placed on landlords of residential property by section 32 of the Housing Act 1961. This requires landlords of residential property let on leases not exceeding seven years to maintain the structure of the building and the principle installations (such as water and electricity), and this is irrespective of any contrary intention displayed by the lease or tenancy agreement. Tenants of business property have had no such protection.

Nor is there any general rule implied by common law that landlords must either put or keep the buildings they have let in good repair. It is true that in 1977 the House of Lords in *Liverpool City Council* v. *Irwin* considered that the Council, as landlord, had an implied obligation to repair the staircases, lifts and rubbish chutes in a block of council flats, but this seems to be of no general application. In the case of *Westminster City Council* v. *Select Management Ltd* (1984)* there was an ingenious and successful plea by the Council against the landlord of a private block of flats that failure to repair common parts of the building was a breach of the provisions of the Health and Safety at Work Act 1974; but to do this the Council had to prove that the common parts of the building qualified as places of work and that the landlords were carrying on a trade or business at the property.

Tenants who are not themselves under full repairing obligations should therefore hold out for adequate repairing covenants by the landlord in those cases where it is already agreed that the tenant's own direct obligations will be limited.

Provisos

Finally in this survey of the contents of the lease, we should look

* Appeal pending

briefly at the 'provisos' which traditionally follow the landlord's covenants. The proviso for suspending rent (in case of fire, etc.) has already been noted. There will also be a proviso for forfeiture of the lease in the event of the tenant's failure to pay rent or to remedy other breaches of covenant or becoming insolvent.

The tenant and his advisers will need to be on the alert for any extra points the landlord may seek to score at this stage. For instance, the landlord may seek to exclude the tenant's right to claim compensation under the Landlord and Tenant Act 1954. After five years of entitlements, this exclusion becomes void. It will therefore be of particular importance in leases which are either due to expire or can be made to expire within a five year period. In such cases, if the landlord regains possession in the prescribed way the tenant would not receive his statutory compensation. At present this is equivalent to the rateable value of the premises times a multiplier – currently 3. After fourteen years the figure is twice the rateable value multiplied by the same factor (i.e. rateable value × 6). After five years the purported exclusion of compensation will not apply *unless* the lease has been assigned to someone who is *not* the successor to the earlier tenant's business. In that case, the five year period starts again. Thus a tenant taking a new fourteen year lease is not likely to feel threatened by the provision, but looking ahead he might argue, 'If I assign the lease in ten years' time to someone carrying on a different trade from me, I might get a lower premium because he will see the possibility of the lease being terminated at the end of the fourteenth year and getting no compensation.'

Break clauses

Of the other provisos that may be found, the most significant would be a 'break' or 'rebuilding' clause. Obviously, if no such thing was discussed at the outset of negotiations then the tenant's solicitor's only proper course is to put a red line straight through it. If it was agreed beforehand, he should be at pains to see that it gives his client reasonable notice. It should be borne in mind that the existence of such a clause and the ability of the landlord to bring the term to a premature end applies to the common law tenancy only. The tenant will still have the protection afforded by the Landlord and Tenant Act, so if the landlord is seeking possession under the terms of this clause, he must still go through the process of serving the required statutory notice as well. If the tenant applies to the court, the landlord must prove compliance with the break clause and with the Landlord and Tenant Act 1954. If, for example, he seeks to rebuild, he must establish a genuine intention to redevelop.

It is at this point that a clause may be inserted excluding the very sections of the Landlord and Tenant Act (sections 24 to 28) which confer the right to a new lease. The clause, if agreed by the parties, need only be a bald statement that they have agreed that these particular sections of the Act will not apply, but it should be borne in mind that such statements will be ineffective unless the parties have obtained a Court Order (in the vast majority of cases by a simple Originating Application to the County Court) authorising the agreement to exclude the above sections.

Guarantees

If the tenants have agreed to provide personal guarantees then, conventionally, it is towards the end of the lease that the surety clause will be located. This imposes upon a third party, who may be one of the directors of the tenant company or perhaps a parent company, the obligation to ensure that the tenant will pay the rent and observe all the other tenant's obligations throughout the term of the lease. Clearly this is an onerous provision but most businessmen will find that as a practical necessity, and unless they are running an established company with a substantial track record, they will not secure the property they require without laying their personal fortunes on the line.

Moreover, the surety remains bound throughout the term and, unless the lease is modified by agreement of the parties, this includes liability for periods after the original tenant has parted with the lease. This extends to increased rent that may be imposed long after the original tenant and its directors have ceased all connection with the property. (See, for example, *Centrovincial Estates* v. *Bulk Storage Ltd* (1983).) The guarantee can even continue after formal expiry of the lease where the tenancy is continuing under section 24(1) of the Landlord and Tenant Act during the period that the tenant has remained in occupation but the terms of the new lease have not yet been fixed either by negotiation or by the court. Whether it does would depend upon the precise wording of the lease: see *GMS Syndicate* v. *Gary Elliott Ltd* (1981) where the guarantor was liable as he had offered a covenant 'during the residue of the term', and *A. Plesser & Co. Ltd* v. *Davis* (1983) where the tenant covenanted to pay the rent 'reserved by the lease' and was found not to be liable during the continuation of the term after the expiry date of the lease.

The usual surety clause

In its most usual form, the surety clause will require the guarantor to take up a lease in his own name in the event of the company going into liquidation. In practice this may not be as useful as it appears because a wily tenant whose company has become insolvent will often have arranged his affairs to ensure that he is of slender means by the time the landlord is ready to enforce his rights under the clause. However, there will clearly be many circumstances in which the ability to insist on a guarantor of substance taking on the lease in his own name will be of considerable worth to the landlord.

As already observed, guarantors should obtain separate advice on their liabilities. They should try to secure the landlord's agreement to the proposition that they should be released from their guarantee if and when the lease is assigned. The landlord may be prepared to concede this so long as it is clear that the guarantee will continue until the lease is assigned to a substantial tenant (for instance, a public company or a private company whose turnover exceeds £x) or until other guarantors of reasonable standing are available to step into the first guarantor's shoes.

Chapter 5

Amendments in red, green and blue

The draft lease the landlord's solicitor prepared will be shuttled to and fro until it is finally agreed. On receipt of the draft the tenant's solicitor will usually make his proposed amendments in red ink. Traditionally, the landlord's solicitor will then respond with any comments or re-amendments in green, and so on. If allowed its head this process can become quite prolonged and it is partly a test of stamina and partly a measure of the relative commercial pressures on each party that will determine which of them gains the most advantage from the exercise.

No erosion of landlord's position

As far as the landlord is concerned, his solicitor should be at pains to see that his client's essential position is not eroded. For instance, where premises are offered on full repairing terms he should defend the basic tenant's obligation to carry out internal and external repairs to the end. Sometimes the property starts off in such poor repair that concessions will be inevitable. The object should then be to give as little ground as possible. If, for example, the landlord agrees to do initial repairs or to allow the tenant a rent free period to carry them out himself, not too much long term damage will be done because the basic tenant's repairing covenant will be left undisturbed for the future. In return for an initial concession the landlord can, in this way, protect his investment and avoid amendments whose side effects could diminish the value of future rent reviews.

Likewise, if the tenant is seeking more freedom of movement in such matters as subletting, changes of use, alterations and so forth, the landlord will want to ensure that he emerges, at the end of the day, with adequate control, even if he has to concede his willingness to act reasonably.

Headlease ties landlord's hands

Where the landlord is not the freeholder his own headlease will dictate, to a considerable extent, how far he is free to make concessions to the tenant. Normally the underlease will aim to duplicate or perhaps improve upon the terms in the landlord's own lease. Clearly, if the headlease contains an absolute covenant against alterations or changing the use of the property the underlease must do the same. The intermediate landlord can offer not to be unreasonable himself, but he can not offer the equivalent concession of his freeholder's behalf without obtaining a variation of the headlease which the freeholder may have no incentive to offer. Moreover, the headlease itself may contain specific requirements dictating the terms on which any sublease is to be granted; for instance, that the sublease must not allow a further subletting of a portion of the premises.

The landlord's primary motive is, of course, to get the property let and to start collecting rent. However, unless he is desperate for revenue the need to create a lease which preserves or enhances his investment will come a very close second. This is why the landlord must always be reluctant to depart from the investor's ideal of an 'FR&I' lease and will try to retain strict control over future alterations to the property or dealings with the lease.

Tenant's primary concern

For the tenant, the primary consideration is likely to be whether anything in the lease is likely to interfere with the proper running of his business. He will also, naturally, be keen to avoid any obligation which looks like adding to the financial burdens for which he has budgeted. Finally, he must ensure that he is not trapped into a long term commitment with no convenient way out. The lease must be reasonably easy to assign, including the right for the original or any incoming tenant to change the nature of the trade or business carried on at the property.

Meeting of parties – and of minds?

Sometimes, although both parties are keen to proceed, their

respective solicitors reach an impasse and it appears that they will exhaust both their clients' patience and their selection of coloured pens without reaching agreement. In such cases a meeting may be the most efficient solution.

There is not much point in a meeting where the bulk of the draft lease still requires detailed examination. At that early point, circulation and amendment of the draft by post or courier is likely to be a more efficient operation than four or more people sitting round a table and wrangling over each of twenty or more pages. However, where the issues have been identified and the parties can concentrate their minds on the three or four vital issues that divide them, then a round table meeting, with solicitors and surveyors present, may well resolve the matter and lead to a swift conclusion of the formalities. A face to face encounter can show each side the other's real priorities and may shame an intransigent party into a more moderate attitude. Indeed, it can be a salutory experience for solicitors to observe their own client in action at such meetings. A meeting helps them to understand their client's requirements as well as providing a forum at which differences with the opposing side may be ironed out.

The parties' surveyors can make a useful contribution to the meeting because, as experienced negotiators, they will be able to advise which of the points at issue are of real relevance. In particular, they can advise on how far clauses in the draft lease and any proposed amendments will have a bearing on management, rent reviews and the value and future marketability of the lease or the freehold. The surveyor is being paid a fee for negotiating the lease: make sure he earns it!

All still 'subject to contract' – but what about costs?

During the period in which the draft leases are involved in this legal version of shuttle diplomacy there would still normally be no legally binding commitment by one party to the other. The solicitors will almost always have taken care to keep the process 'subject to contract' and to insist that the letters and documents initiated by them do not bind their clients in any way.

An exception to this practice may be the question of the landlord's solicitor's costs. It is the practice of a number of firms acting for landlords to ask the tenant's solicitor to provide a professional undertaking at the outset of the transaction that he will 'meet the landlord's costs whether or not the matter proceeds'. This ploy may well work in a bullish property market where the tenant is very anxious to secure the property. To give a personal undertaking of this kind, the tenant's solicitor must either be very sure of his client or take enough money from him in advance to ensure that he can meet the landlord's costs and honour his undertaking at his client's rather than his own expense. Even if he feels obliged to agree, the tenant's solicitor should make it clear that his client does not agree to meet the costs if the transaction aborts due to some default of the landlord.

My own impression is that this practice is less prevalent now than it used to be. If an undertaking is requested, the tenant's solicitors usually respond by indicating their client's willingness to meet the landlord's 'reasonable legal costs' if and when the matter is completed, but not otherwise.

Good faith; on both sides?

As it will be some time before either side is contractually bound, it is reasonable for each party to expect from the other some evidence of commitment to the proposed lease. Ideally, a landlord might wish to take a non-returnable deposit but most tenants would naturally resist. If the deposit is made returnable, though, its payment is really a meaningless gesture. The fact that the tenant instructs his solicitors and arranges a structural survey is probably a better indication that he is not a time waster and is seriously intending to take the property.

For the tenant, the best evidence of the landlord's good faith is his withdrawal of the property from active marketing. However, the landlord's surveyors will usually be reluctant to advise this because of the inevitable delay that can arise in finding a new applicant if a letting proves to be abortive. Moreover, other potential tenants may feel 'something must be wrong with the property' if it becomes known in the market that an earlier attempted letting failed.

Powers to sign

Whether round a table or by correspondence between solicitors, an agreement could be reached in principle; then one client's represent-ative will say that before anything binding can be signed he must obtain the approval of his head office or his board of directors. It is therefore essential to establish whether the individuals who are purporting to represent the landlord or the tenant have the power to bind their principals or sign agreements on their behalf. Otherwise, frustrating delays can occur whilst reports are submitted to head office or everyone waits for the next board meeting. The position can be aggravated further if the landlord or the tenant is a subsidiary of a foreign company and major policy decisions have to be referred abroad.

Absence of internal consent can also be a problem if someone at head office comes up with an objection that a certain point 'is not head office policy', or it may simply be a case of a senior executive or director trying to justify his existence. The moral is to make sure at the outset that the parties to a negotiation have the necessary authority to commit the company they represent. Tactful but firm enquiries will pay off in such circumstances.

Chapter 6

Concluding the deal

The parties and their solicitors have finally agreed the wording of the draft lease. They are now on the point of achieving the culmination of the efforts of the past days, weeks or even months of patient negotiations.

Engrossments are prepared

Conventionally what will now happen is that the landlord's solicitor, who is in possession of the draft lease containing all the agreed amendments and re-amendments, will prepare 'the engrossments', i.e. two properly typed and (hopefully) identical copies of the lease, normally on stout paper and sewn up or securely bound. The original lease requires the landlord's seal or signature and the counterpart lease must be signed by the tenant and by the surety, if there is one. If there are any discrepancies between the original and the counterpart, then the wording of the original lease takes precedence.

What will normally happen is that the landlord's solicitor will submit the counterpart lease to his opposite number for signature by the tenant and will at the same time submit his account (assuming that the tenant has agreed to pay it) together with a demand for any initial rent that will be payable on completion of the lease. He will send the original lease to his client and after it has been executed by the landlord he will hold it in his file to await formal completion.

Completion

This will normally take place when the counterpart lease is received together with a cheque for whatever sum is due to the landlord or his solicitors and, more often than not, completion is effected through the post.

A last-minute change of heart

An interesting point can arise when the parties change their minds at the last minute. Suppose an agreement of the kind mentioned has not been signed, but each party has not only received the lease for signature but has actually signed it. The landlord and tenant have returned the original and counterpart leases to their respective solicitors but at the last moment one of them decides not to proceed. Can they change their minds at this late stage? There is, of course, an agreed form of lease but the correspondence between the parties and their advisers is probably stated to be 'subject to contract'. On the other hand, they have actually executed the documents by solemnly applying their hands and seals or company seals as the case may be. Does the mere absence of a formal exchange of documents prevent the tenancy from coming into being?

There has been some case law about the precise point in time at which the parties are actually bound. As a physical necessity both the lease and the counterpart will have been executed (signed and sealed) by each of the parties a few days or even several weeks before completion, namely formal exchange of leases, takes place. Where a document has been solemnly executed but is not intended to take effect until the occurrence of a certain event (e.g. payment of rent, signature of counterpart) this is called 'an escrow'. In *Alan Estates Ltd* v. *W.G. Stores Ltd* (1982) the Court of Appeal considered that a lease delivered as an escrow took effect from the date of delivery not from the date the condition was fulfilled. So it may be difficult for a landlord or tenant who is in two minds about whether to proceed with a letting to withdraw once he has sealed and signed the lease.

Sealing by limited companies

The problem seems most likely to arise where the party concerned is a limited company, because it would normally have passed a suitable resolution to execute the document and 'delivery' has been held by the courts to include delivery to the company's own solicitor

(*Vincent* v. *Premo Enterprises (Voucher Sales) Ltd* (1969)). However, it does seem open to the landlord to qualify the manner in
which the lease is executed so as to make it clear that he does not
intend to be bound until the specified event has taken place (*Pattle*
v. *Hornibrook* (1897)) and in practice it seems reasonable to assume
that the landlord does post the executed lease to his own solicitor on
this understanding.

It seems that the parties will almost certainly be bound if they
have carried out some act referable to the tenancy; for instance, if
the tenant has paid some rent or gone into physical residence or at
least started work on the property. On the landlord's part, handing
over the keys to the tenant (without some express declaration that
they were on loan) would make it very difficult for the landlord to
withdraw.

Generally, therefore, the parties are not bound until the point at
which the landlord's solicitor posts the original lease, signed by his
client and duly dated, to the tenant's solicitor.

Filling in the blanks

Because he is the person who will be effecting the formal exchange
(where completion is taking place through the post), the landlord's
solicitor must be meticulous in filling in the various blank spaces in
both the original and the counterpart lease. Not only must the date
of exchange be completed, but also the date from which the tenant
will first become liable to pay rent. Where a rent free period was
agreed, this date may be several weeks or months after the lease
itself is dated. On the other hand, where the tenant has been
allowed access to the property before completion of the legal
formalities, rent may have become payable from a date preceding
the formal grant of the lease.

Once the documents are exchanged and any rent and costs due
from the tenant have been collected, the landlord's solicitor will
advise his client (or the agent) that completion has taken place. If
access has not already been granted, the keys can now be released
and the tenant can move in.

Is an agreement as good as a lease?

So far so good. But there are now many possible variations to this simple conventional procedure. The main one will be where the parties are in a great hurry to complete. Anyone studying property law is taught at an early stage that 'an agreement for a lease is as good as a lease' (*Walsh* v. *Lonsdale* (1882)), and if the parties are in a hurry they can take advantage of this well established principle. So long as the draft lease is agreed, there is sufficient certainty of terms to form an agreement.

The agreement can conveniently be contained in an exchange of letters between the parties or their solicitors. For instance the tenant's solicitors might write to the landlord or his solicitor stating:

> 'We enclose our cheque for £1,000 representing the first quarter's rent and if you will allow our clients into possession of the premises on the terms set out in the agreed form of lease we undertake that they will execute the counterpart lease in its agreed form within fourteen days of it being presented for signature and that they will take up the completed lease executed by your clients.'

For the agreement to be binding, the landlord's solicitor must signify his unconditional acceptance of these terms on his client's behalf.

If an agreement of this kind is concluded, then even though there will be a delay between agreement to the wording of the draft lease and its formal signature and exchange the agreement will, for practical purposes, protect the parties. Nevertheless, it is always desirable that the lease itself should be granted because the agreement will be of an equitable nature only.

If the landlord sells his interest and the tenant has failed to register his interest as an estate contract at the Land Registry or Land Charges Registry, the agreement would be void against a purchaser for 'money or money's worth' (Land Charges Act 1972 section 4(6)). The landlord would not be able to enforce the tenant's covenants if the agreement had been assigned to a new tenant. Such agreements should therefore be made non-assignable, i.e. personal to the original tenant.

Separate agreement

In Chapter 2, I considered those cases where the parties will have decided to enter into a separate contract or agreement for lease and where, for some sufficient reason, there will be some delay between signature of agreement in principle (which will embody an agreed draft lease) and completion of the lease itself. Most commonly this will be where building works have to be carried out (by the landlord or by the tenant) before the lease can be granted, but it may simply be because the landlord is not ready to let or the tenant is not ready to take the premises until a later specified date.

Where there is to be any significant delay the tenant, in particular, should ensure that the solicitor has taken the necessary steps to register his interest as 'an estate contract' either at the Land Charges Registry or, if applicable, at the Land Registry itself. This ensures that anyone attempting to purchase the property (or take a lease thereof) will be deemed to have notice of the tenant's interest and will be bound by it whether or not he has actual knowledge. As the converse position is that if the tenant's interest is not registered any potential purchaser or mortgagee can disregard the tenant's interest, the need for such registration is only too apparent.

Conditions of sale

Where there has been a prior agreement it will very often incorporate one of the standard forms of conditions of sale (e.g. the Law Society's Conditions or the National Conditions), just as in the case of a contract for the sale of freehold property. These conditions regulate such questions as whether one party is in default and can serve notice on the other, following which the contract could be rescinded and damages claimed.

But what is the position if the parties have relied on correspondence and have not incorporated any special conditions? In that case the parties are treated as having entered into an 'open contract' to which certain conditions are implied either by the Law of Property Act 1925 or by common law. For example, time is not of the essence of such a contract so any time limits specified in a contract resting on correspondence will not be strictly enforceable. If a tenant refused to complete a lease the landlord would, on general principles, have to give the tenant reasonable advance notice that if he did not complete by a certain date the landlord would choose to treat the contract as rescinded. This contrasts with the case where the National or Law Society's Conditions are employed where the contract can be rescinded after a precise period of notice; sixteen working days in the case of the National Conditions, and fifteen working days in the case of the Law Society's Conditions.

We will now assume that the parties have complied with their obligations and that the lease is duly completed. Any necessary stamping and registration formalities will be attended to by the lawyers; the tenant will now be in occupation and paying rent. The following chapters will consider the events that can occur in the course of the tenancy.

Chapter 7

Changes of circumstance

A lease can run for a term of a few months or for up to twenty-five years or more. During that time a variety of events may occur which will require the tenant to approach the landlord for his consent. Of these, the most common will be applications to assign the lease, create underlettings, change the permitted use and carry out alterations. It may well be that the landlord will be asked to consider a combination of such requests. In some cases the lease may already have prescribed a formula catering for the tenant's request. The wording of the lease may, as we have seen in Chapter 4, be modified by the Landlord and Tenant Act 1927 (section 19(1) on assigning and subletting, section 19(2) on alterations and section 19(3) on changes of use). Even if the lease or the legislation is silent, there is nothing to stop the parties varying the terms of the lease by mutual agreement and 'at arm's length'.

Although it will be quite common for the tenant, who may be selling his lease to someone proposing to carry on a different kind of business, to request his landlord's consent to an assignment, a change of use and to alterations, let us for simplicity look at them separately.

Assigning the lease

Assigning simply means that you want to sell or transfer your interest in the lease. The tenant proposing to dispose of his premises should look at the lease or ask his solicitor to do so and pass on his conclusions to the agent that he has instructed so that they can establish, at the outset, what the landlord's requirements are likely to be. If the lease is completely silent on the point the tenant can deal with the premises at will without seeking the landlord's approval (*Bruerton* v. *Rainsford* (1583)). In modern times, this is extremely unusual.

Almost every modern lease will prohibit absolutely the right 'to assign part', i.e. to sell a portion of the building only. Obviously, this is undesirable from the landlord's viewpoint because it means he must collect his rent from two tenants rather than one and there could be arguments over how the rent should be apportioned between the tenants. A tenant who wishes to retain part of his premises but dispose of the remainder will normally have to proceed by way of a subletting (see below).

Absolute bar on assignment

It would not be unusual to find a lease which contains an absolute prohibition on assignment. This often happens where a lease is only for a short term or where the landlord is adamant that he must have absolute control of the premises. Hopefully, a tenant holding such a lease was properly advised at the outset and knew what he was signing, but if he finds that he is holding a lease of this nature then his right to sell is completely in the hands of the landlord. Unless the landlord feels inclined to agree, the original tenant is saddled with the lease until it expires.

If the tenant does, however, assign the lease without consent, the assignment will be valid and the assignee will become the new tenant but the landlord will immediately have the right to forfeit the lease and the new tenant will be forced to ask the court for relief, which he might not get in view of the flagrant breach of covenant.

Where a tenant is saddled with a long lease which he wishes to assign, all may not be lost. If there are periodic rent reviews he should point out to his landlord that the absolute bar on assigning the lease can have a disastrous effect on the rent the landlord will get when the rent reviews arrive. This point alone may be sufficient to persuade the landlord to relent, and not merely to allow the assignment but to agree to a variation of the lease so as to allow future assignments with his consent which he will not unreasonably withhold. Even where the lease is a short one, the tenant should direct his landlord's attention to the likelihood that if the restriction on assigning is not relaxed the court will order a lower rent when the lease is renewed under the Landlord and Tenant Act 1954.

The normal qualified covenant

Fortunately, such a prohibition is most unusual. Instead of an 'absolute' covenant against assigning, what is more usual is to find a 'qualified' covenant which allows the tenant to assign his lease provided he obtains the landlord's consent. Once those words are contained in a lease it is implied by statute (section 19(1) of the Landlord and Tenant Act 1927) that the landlord must not be unreasonable in refusing consent.

However, even if the landlord's obligation to be reasonable is expressly stated in the lease, the right to assign may still be hedged around with various restrictions and requirements. For instance, the lease may state that if the assignment is made to a limited company then it will be not permitted until one or more of its directors enters into a personal covenant with the landlord. This can cause problems where the new tenant is a major public company. The practical effect is, therefore, that a tenant who has decided to sell his lease should satisfy himself at the outset as to what his landlord is likely to require.

References

As the landlord's consent will almost certainly be needed he, or his agents, should arrange to take up the usual references to prove that the new tenant is likely to be respectable and able to pay the rent. A banker's reference will always be required and a solicitor's and an accountant's will normally be expected as well. In addition, the landlord would usually like to see a reference from the tenant's present landlord (if he has one) and trade references supplied by businesses which have had dealings with the new tenant.

It is at this point that time will be saved if the need to supply directors' guarantees is anticipated by asking the proposed new tenant to supply the names of such directors and the names of bankers and other referees for them as well.

There is no universal practice as to who should take up these references. Sometimes it is the selling agent. Sometimes it is the tenant's solicitor. Sometimes the agents or solicitors acting for the new tenant, or assignee, take up the references. Normally, the landlord expects to be presented with a set of reference letters, not merely a set of names to whom he is expected to write himself. It is, of course, important that the questions addressed to the referees should be accurate; in particular they should quote the correct rental, and if there are any service charges of substance the approximate figure should be mentioned as well.

Bank references

It should be borne in mind that banks do not normally accept reference enquiries except from other banks, so you have to ask your own bank to make the enquiry. A typical request for a bank reference would be:

> Clients of ours are proposing to assign to Bloggs Limited of 45 High Street, Castletown, a lease of business premises at an annual rent of £5,000 plus service charges of £250.
> Will you please take up a reference with their bankers, Lloyds Bank, High Street, Castletown, and enquire if they would make respectable and responsible leaseholders of business premises, able to pay the above rental.

If you are lucky, you will get the reply 'good for the figure and purpose of your enquiry' or, if you are very lucky, 'undoubted'. You have to read between the lines if the reference supplied is slightly evasive, such as 'respectable and trustworthy but we cannot speak for the figures mentioned'.

References given by professional firms will almost always be qualified with a disclaimer that the person giving the reference is doing so without liability on the part of his firm or its partners. Indeed, anyone giving such a reference should be circumspect in this matter because, even if he has no contract with the person relying on it, he could be liable in negligence.

The possibility of a claim for negligence was established by one of the most famous cases of recent times, *Hedley Byrne & Co. Ltd* v. *Heller & Partners Ltd* (1963). This and a line of subsequent cases makes it clear that if reliance is placed on a representation given negligently the person giving it can be liable in damages.

There are also special rules relating to credit reference agencies as defined by the Consumer Credit Act 1974. Organisations which provide information about creditworthiness as a business activity in itself have to be licensed and can be required to disclose their files to the person who is the subject of the enquiry. The Act does not apply to solicitors, accountants, banks, surveyors and traders for whom the provision of references is a service incidental to their other activities.

How to be reasonable

Once the references are in they will be presented to the landlord or his advisers and, as we have seen, he will usually be obliged to be reasonable about giving consent. This means he must have regard to the nature and type of premises which are being let. He cannot expect a gilt-edged tenant for a slum property.

In considering whether a landlord is being reasonable, the court will look at each situation according to its own particular facts. The landlord must not refuse consent in order to gain an advantage for himself. In *Bromley Park Garden Estate Ltd* v. *Moss* (1982) the landlords hoped that by blocking the request of a residential tenant to assign his lease of a flat over a shop they would force him to surrender it and allow them to grant the lease of the whole building to the commercial tenant downstairs. The landlord was considered to be acting unreasonably. But it does seem reasonable to refuse licence to assign where the effect of assigning would be to bring a tenancy under the control of the Rent Act or Part II of the Landlord and Tenant Act where such protection did not apply before (*West Layton Ltd* v. *Ford* (1979)). The tenant is nevertheless obliged to ask for consent; even if the assignee would obviously be an excellent tenant, assigning without bothering to request consent makes the lease liable for forfeiture.

The tenant seeking to assign his lease must be realistic about the chances of an assignment going through. There are many people with little business experience (for example those in receipt of a redundancy payment) looking to start up new businesses and, without a track record or a guarantee from an experienced business-man, such a person may simply not be acceptable to the landlord.

Pre-emption clauses

One restriction that is sometimes found is a 'pre-emption clause', namely the requirement that the tenant must first offer the premises to the landlord before offering them elsewhere. The landlord is usually given a fixed time, say twenty-eight days, to exercise his right to take the premises back. He may be able to do so with or without a premium.

A landlord seeking to impose such a clause is, however, stepping on to a legal minefield. On the one hand, he might think that clause 19 of the 1927 Landlord and Tenant Act (requiring consent not to be unreasonably withheld) might render a pre-emption clause ineffective. In *Adler* v. *Upper Grosvenor Street Investment Ltd* (1957), the court said that the offer to surrender was a step to be taken before the question of consent arose, so the clause seemed to be valid and binding. But in 1974 in *Greene* v. *Church Commissioners for England* it was shown that to be valid against assignees of the lease (as opposed to the original tenant) the pre-emption clause had to be registered as an estate contract at the Land Charges Registry (or the Land Registry in the case of registered land).

Even then the landlord is not out of the woods. The clause, like any other contract to surrender, purports to contract out of the protection of the Landlord and Tenant Act 1954 and section 38 of that Act makes the offer of surrender unenforceable. As we will see in Chapter 10, the parties must make a joint application to the court to contract out of the Act. In *Allnatt London Properties Ltd* v. *Newton* (1984) the Court of Appeal held that a pre-emption clause did have 'the effect of precluding the tenant' from applying for a new tenancy under the 1954 Act and left the tenant in the position that he could not assign and the landlord in the position that he could not enforce the surrender.

So it would seem that for business tenants clauses of this kind in their leases can be ignored unless (a) at the time the lease was granted the parties obtained a court order to contract out of the renewal provisions of the 1954 Act and (b) the tenant is either the original lessee or, if he is not, the landlord had already registered the clause as an estate contract before the tenant took over the lease.

Notwithstanding *Allnatt* v. *Newton*, there is nothing to prevent the parties *operating* the 'surrender back' clause. The problem is that the parties can not bind one another in advance to proceed with the surrender or agree to a dealing.

Continuing obligations

The tenant must remember that when he transfers his interest to an assignee his liabilities are not, alas, at an end. As we saw in Chapter 1, an original lessee is bound to his landlord by 'privity of contract' throughout the remainder of the term. Even when the rent is reviewed after he has assigned the lease, the original tenant can be pursued to pay the increased rent although he had nothing to do with the review negotiations.

If the tenant is not the original lessee, then the basic rule is that he ceases to be liable to the landlord once he has got rid of the lease by a further assignment. In practice, however, this is often not the case, because before taking over the lease the tenant will have been asked to add his signature to the licence permitting the assignment. That document may well contain a direct covenant with the landlord that the new tenant will perform the tenant's covenants and pay the rent 'for the residue of the term'.

It follows that it is not only in the landlord's interest but also vital for the tenant to see that his successor is of sufficient substance to meet his obligations under the lease. If he is in any doubt he should not assign but sublet. That way, if the subtenant defaults he does at least get the premises back.

Subletting

Many of the observations about assignment, including references and the landlord's obligation to be reasonable, apply to underletting as well. Once more, the tenant and his agents should look at the lease at the outset of the transaction. For instance, it may say that subletting of part of the property is prohibited. In such circumstances the tenant of a four-storey building may find himself unable to sublet, say, the shop portion alone or the first and second floors on their own. Or it may be that the lease does allow subletting of part but only once or only in complete floors. There is no point in the tenant wasting time on a project to which the landlord need never consent. If it is vital for him to sublet part only, he may have to approach the landlord and re-negotiate the lease and, perhaps, pay a penalty such as a single payment or a continuing licence fee for the privilege. (Where there is an absolute restriction, such payments do *not* contravene section 19(1) of the Landlord and Tenant Act 1927.)

Even if underletting the whole or the desired portion of the building is acceptable, the lease may still make certain stipulations. For instance, a prudent landlord will have insisted that the subletting must be at the current rack rental. This is to protect the landlord from the danger that a tenant might try to sell a sublease at a high premium but a low rent; the tenant himself might then abscond or go out of business leaving the landlord with a subtenant unable or unwilling to pay the full rent. The tenant's lease (or 'headlease' as it will be in this context) may also insist that any underlease must have rent reviews on precisely the same basis as those in the headlease. It may well also require similar covenants to the headlease to be imposed in the underlease, although this may not be strictly practicable when only part of the building is being sublet.

The underlease can, of course, be for any term up to the length of the tenant's own headlease but a nominal 'reversion' of two or three days is normally deducted from the length of the term of the headlease. There are two main reasons why this is necessary. First, a nominal reversion must be retained because a subletting for the whole of the tenant's term takes effect in law as an assignment (*Parmenter* v. *Webber* (1818)). Secondly, the reversion enables the tenant to sue for forfeiture and to claim damages against his tenant in respect of the reversion itself.

Can the landlord retain his competence?

In the case of business premises, a landlord is no longer the 'competent landlord' for the purpose of operating the renewal provisions of the Landlord and Tenant Act 1954 if, when his subtenant is due to renew his lease, there is less than fourteen months to run of the headlease. Where the landlord wishes to retain the power to claim a new headlease for himself and thereafter to occupy the property, he should therefore ensure that he grants an underlease at least fourteen months less in duration than his own headlease. To regain occupation and claim a new lease for himself he would have to arrange for the sublease to be contracted out of the renewal provisions of the Act. Alternatively, he would have to claim possession against the subtenant on the grounds that he requires the premises for his own occupation. In those circumstances, the initial term of the sublease would have to be at least five years.

Practice varies as to whether the landlord or his solicitors will actually want to see the underlease in its final form before it is actually granted. Mostly they will restrict themselves to granting a licence specifying their requirements and will not see the underlease itself until it is produced for 'registration' after it is completed.

Sharing

Where the lease contains a clause prohibiting the tenant from 'parting with possession' but does not prohibit sharing, this does not prevent the tenant granting an interest which does not give 'possession' but merely allows 'occupation'. This opens the way for the tenant to grant occupation licences or to put in a 'manager' who pays a share of his profits or his turnover to the tenant.

Alterations

A tenant may want to carry out alterations for his own benefit or it may be a new subtenant or assignee who wishes to alter the premises to suit his requirements. In either case reference must be made once more to the lease to see whether alterations are permitted at all or under certain conditions.

It is not unusual to find a complete prohibition on any alterations, in which case such matters are entirely at the landlord's discretion. Sometimes certain types of alterations, such as structural works, are prohibited but internal decorative or non-structural works permitted; sometimes they need consent and sometimes not.

Where the covenant is 'qualified' and not 'absolute' (i.e. where alterations of some kind are permitted with landlord's consent) then, if the lease does not insist on the landlord being reasonable, the Landlord and Tenant Act 1927 again comes to the tenant's assistance. However, in this case (section 19(2)) there is an important difference compared to the provisions we looked at earlier regarding assigning and subletting. There, in any such case, the landlord was bound not to unreasonably withhold his consent. In the case of alterations, the landlord's obligation to be reasonable (if it is not spelled out in the lease) is restricted to alterations which amount to 'improvements'. What is an improvement is normally considered from the viewpoint of the tenant. The landlord may still be entitled to ask for compensation if any adjoining building of his is diminished in value or, if the improvement does not add to the ultimate letting value, the landlord may be entitled to ask the tenant to reinstate the property to its earlier condition when the lease comes to an end.

Improvements

Where improvements are to be carried out there are important implications both for the landlord and the tenant. Future rent on review or renewal and the tenant's right to compensation may all be affected. Care should be taken not to confuse the law and its requirements as it affects:

(a) rent on review,
(b) rent on renewal, and
(c) compensation for improvements.

A different body of law applies to each category so different responses are required from the parties, as we shall see below.

Implications on renewal

The treatment of improvements when leases are renewed under the 1954 Act is governed by section 34(1)(c) as amended by section 1 of the Law of Property Act 1969. That section requires the court to disregard 'any effect on rent of an improvement to which this paragraph applies'. It is important to read the section in its amended form with great care because common misconceptions have arisen over the so called 'twenty-one year rule'. The improvement will be disregarded for rental purposes on renewal if it is not pursuant to an obligation to the *immediate* landlord and is carried out by a *tenant* (so NB subtenants' improvements are not covered) and *either* it was carried out during the current tenancy, i.e. the one that is being renewed (note that so long as it is the current tenancy there is no time limit but improvements effected before grant of the lease under some earlier licence or occupation agreement would not qualify), *or* it was completed within twenty-one years of the tenant's application to the court for a new tenancy *and* there was a business tenancy covered by section 23(1) in existence throughout that period *and* there has been no break in the relationship of landlord and tenant.

Implications on compensation for improvements

If the tenant is to preserve his right to claim compensation for improvements when his lease comes to an end (in the event that the tenant's application for a new tenancy is refused), he must follow the correct procedure at this stage. This is laid down by sections 1 to 3 of the Landlord and Tenant Act 1927. These provide that the tenant must serve notice on the landlord of his intention to carry out the improvement and regulate the requirements the landlord may impose. They also give the landlord the option of carrying out the work himself and of charging a reasonable increase in rent.

The tenant will qualify for compensation from the landlord if the tenant has carried out the correct procedure and if, at the end of the tenancy, the landlord successfully opposes his right to renew (see Chapter 10). This compensation will be the lesser of (a) the addition in value to the 'holding' as a direct result of the improvements, *or* (b) the cost of carrying out the improvements at the end of the tenancy but deducting costs of repair which are covered by the tenant's normal repairing covenant.

Tenants should remember that even if they go through the proper notice procedure at the time of the improvements they will not receive compensation if the landlord offers a new lease at the end of the term (although the rent may 'disregard' the improvement, as indicated above). Nor will the tenant get compensation if the landlord intends to demolish because normally the improvement will not have added to the value of the landlord's holding.

In all three cases (review, renewal and compensation) it is essential that the tenant ensures the landlord grants his consent in a form that *permits* the improvement: if it imposes an *obligation* to improve the tenant will not, after all, be given credit for the improvements.

On a practical level, proposals for alterations are often dealt with on an informal basis; for instance, an exchange of letters between the landlord and the tenant or the production of plans by the tenant's builder or surveyor on which the landlord or his representatives will merely endorse their approval. The need for the grant of a formal licence for alterations will arise where the landlord wants to impose certain conditions, such as a requirement to reinstate the premises (as mentioned above), or perhaps the imposition of a time limit within which the works are to be carried out, a requirement that a consent will be subject to the tenant obtaining planning permission and so forth.

Changes of use

A tenant will sometimes want to vary or extend his business activities at his existing premises or, if he is disposing of his lease, he may find his purchaser wishes to carry on a different kind of business from himself. In both cases the landlord's consent will almost invariably be required.

Traditionally, landlords liked to impose strict user clauses, e.g. 'not to use the premises except as a retail newsagent and confectioner'. It was then a matter of negotiation as to whether the tenant's solicitor could persuade the landlord's solicitor to relax this provision so that other uses would be permitted with the landlord's consent and to provide that such a consent would not be unreasonably withheld.

However, the rise of the rent review industry and the expertise of valuers advising landlords has resulted in landlords realising that they will often get a better rent, both on review and on renewal, if a fairly 'open user' clause is incorporated in the lease. For this reason many modern leases, whilst specifying a particular trade, will allow different trades (perhaps within a particular planning category) with landlord's consent. Once again, where the landlord is obliged not to be unreasonable the courts have held that it is unreasonable for the landlord to use the situation to gain a collateral advantage for himself. In *Anglia Building Society* v. *Sheffield City Council* (1983) the landlord had opposed Anglia's request to use as a building society office a property which had previously been in use as an employment agency. The landlord (Sheffield City Council) would have liked to see a retail use and brought evidence to show that retail use would yield a higher rent. The Court of Appeal decided that the lease already permitted a service as well as retail use and there was no evidence that building society use would be detrimental compared with what had already been permitted. The Council was not entitled to apply the criteria appropriate to a planning authority whilst wearing its landlord's hat.

Reasonableness not implied

Where the words 'not to be unreasonably withheld' are not spelled out, section 19(3) of the Landlord and Tenant Act 1927 is not quite as helpful to the tenant as sections 19(1) and (2) because it does not imply those words automatically. Instead, it simply states that where the consent of the landlord is required to a change of use, a landlord cannot demand a financial penalty by increasing the rent or charging a premium although he can ask for a reasonable sum if he thinks that his property (or neighbouring property) will be diminished in value. Landlords can, however, escape from this provision merely by refusing their consent and waiting for (but not demanding) an offer.

It has been argued by reference to the case of *Bocardo S.A.* v. *S. & M. Hotels Ltd* (1980) that, even though section 19(3) of the Landlord and Tenant Act 1927 does not say that consent to changes of use is not to be unreasonably withheld, the courts should still interpret the Act as if that provision were implied. However, the High Court rejected that argument in the case of *Guardian Assurance Co. Ltd* v. *Gants Hill Holdings Ltd* (1983). Cogent arguments were advanced in both cases and it is by no means certain how the Court of Appeal would decide the matter. In the absence of an 'open user' clause a tenant assigning his lease to a purchaser carrying on a different business from himself should, therefore, be sure to investigate the landlord's willingness to allow the new trade to be carried on at the premises, and the same remarks apply to any new trade he wishes to carry on himself.

It should be added that even if alterations of business use are permitted within limits most leases will still carry a list of activities which are expressly prohibited. For instance, many landlords of commercial property are fearful of the effect of the Rent Acts and will absolutely prohibit any residential use of any proportion of the property, even if a building was originally designed to have some residential content. Older leases will often outlaw exotic trades such as soap boilers and tallow chandlers, and use of the buildings as a lunatic asylum. More recently, use as a sex shop or the sale of pornographic material may be prohibited. In those cases, of course, the criterion of reasonableness does not apply and any variation is in the landlord's discretion.

Remedies for landlord's refusal

What happens if the landlord is adamant and refuses to agree to a tenant requesting the consents discussed in this chapter? If the prohibition in the lease is an absolute one and the tenant goes ahead regardless, he will be liable to forfeiture of his lease (see Chapter 8) and will endanger his position perhaps irretrievably. If the covenant is, however, a qualified one and if reasonableness is either spelled out in the lease or implied by statute then the tenant has two alternatives.

He can simply go ahead with the proposed course of action, and if the landlord then sues him for forfeiture of the lease he will be able to use the landlord's unreasonableness as a defence. In some cases this will be a matter of bluff; the tenant may calculate that the landlord will not bother to introduce the necessary proceedings. It will, however, be for the tenant to persuade the court that the landlord was unreasonable. Despite the uncertainty, it may well be that commercial necessity will persuade the tenant to proceed with his proposals in the case of unreasonable refusal by the landlord. Whether it is sensible to take this course may depend on the degree of financial risk involved. A prospective assignee or purchaser proposing to invest substantial sums in the property would be unlikely to run the risk.

The more prudent course is to ask the court for a declaration that the landlord is being unreasonable. This declaration will be to the High Court or, where the premises have a rateable value below a certain figure (currently £5,000), to the County Court. If the landlord is being unreasonable, the threat to apply for such a declaration is often sufficient to persuade him to disgorge the necessary licence!

In practice, on the other hand, the delay caused by the landlord's refusal and the inevitable delays in getting the point heard by the court will often result in the deal falling through simply because the tenant is not prepared to wait. The tenant can not claim damages if the landlord unreasonably refuses consent to an assignment or subletting (*Treloar* v. *Bigge* (1874)) except in the unusual event that his obligation to be reasonable is contained in a landlord's covenant.

Chapter 8

Breaches of covenant

Like true love, the course of the average commercial lease (almost) never did run smooth. We have already seen that many of the twenty or more pages which comprise the lease will be taken up with a list of covenants; most by the tenant, some by the landlord. It is, therefore, more than likely that during the term of the lease one party will consider that the other has broken one or more of the promises contained in those covenants.

Non-payment of rent

Because he has made so many more promises than the landlord it is likely to be the tenant who is in breach, and by far the most significant and obvious breach will be his failure to pay the rent. We should consider this first of all, not only because of its obvious importance but also because of the significant differences in remedy between the breaches of covenant to pay rent and other breaches of covenant.

First, when does the breach of that covenant occur? Commercial rents are almost always payable in advance and they are therefore due on the stated date, usually one of the four legal Quarter Days: 25 March, 24 June, 29 September and 25 December. (Everyone can remember Christmas Day. The easy way to remember the others is that you add to 20 the number of letters in the month.) It follows that the rent is overdue if it is only one day late.

Many leases now require the tenant to pay interest when the rent becomes overdue. A distinction must be made between a lease which says that the interest starts running immediately and those which say that it starts from fourteen or perhaps twenty-one days later.

Distress

This is not just a description of the feelings of the unpaid landlord or
the harassed tenant, but a long-standing legal remedy available to
any landlord whose tenant has failed to pay. It is, in short, the
power to send in the bailiffs. Many people may be under the
impression that you have to sign judgment before sending in the
bailiffs but this is not so in the case of non-payment of rent. As a
practical proposition many landlords elect to instruct certificated
bailiffs who, given a short formal note of instructions and brief
details of the lease and the arrears, will present themselves at the
premises and threaten to take away and dispose of the tenant's
goods unless payment of the outstanding rent is effected forthwith.

For the landlord this is often a quick and effective way of bringing
a tenant into line but it carries the penalty that the bailiffs' fees
cannot be passed on to the tenant (as would be the case with the
expenses of a court bailiff acting on a judgment). Instead, the fee
(usually 10%) must be deducted from the rent recovered. Under the
Distress for Rent Rules, the bailiff can only distrain for a relatively
small sum in addition to the rent that is due, so it is the landlord who
bears the expense.

If the tenant is not personally in possession but has subtenants at
the property, then under the Distress for Rent (Amendment) Act
1906 the landlord can serve notice on the subtenants that they must
pay their rent to him direct until the arrears of their immediate
landlord have been cleared.

The landlord does not automatically have everything his own
way. The tenant may have a legitimate objection to the landlord's
claim; for instance, he may already have paid, he may be entitled to
a rent free period, or the landlord may have miscalculated.
Moreover, the tenant may be able to allege that the landlord is
himself in breach of covenant and that he has a counter claim for
damages which could exceed the rent that is due. In such cases the
tenant's remedy in order to fend off the action of the certificated
bailiff is to apply by summons either to the County Court or to the
High Court for a declaration preventing the bailiff from distraining
on his property until the legal issues have been properly litigated. So
long as the tenant can show a prima facie case he can effectively put
a spoke in the landlord's wheel, but of course if the tenant's
objection is purely vexatious he will merely have bought a limited
amount of time before the bailiffs return and will, moreover, risk

having to pay all the costs of the litigation.

Some goods are safe from the bailiff's clutches. Fixtures are exempt, even if as between landlord and tenant they qualify as tenant's fixtures. Nor must the bailiff take perishables or goods in actual use. Bedding, wearing apparel and implements of trade are exempt to a value of £50 and thereafter may only be taken if there are insufficient goods of other categories to cover the unpaid rent. Goods on hire purchase and most categories of goods belonging to a third party may not be taken. Finally, the bailiff may not distrain between dusk and dawn nor on a Sunday.

Action to recover rent

Rent is a debt like any other and can be recovered by action in the High Court or the County Court just as any other money due under a contract can be.

If the amount due exceeds £5,000 action must be taken in the High Court because the County Court has no jurisdiction to deal with sums above that figure (unless the litigants agree). Although the claim for sums below £5,000 should normally be made in the County Court, landlords claiming a lesser sum will often do so by issuing a High Court Writ rather than a County Court Summons. This is because there is a relatively simple High Court procedure (under Order 14 of the Rules of the Supreme Court) which allows the plaintiff (the landlord, in this case) to sign judgment very quickly where there is clearly no defence. As soon as the writ is issued and acknowledged, his solicitors can take out a summons before a High Court Master. The landlord swears a short affidavit to say there is no defence to his claim and unless the tenant can prove, by filing his own affidavit, that there actually is a defence, the landlord will get his judgment immediately the summons is heard. This can sometimes be faster and more effective than proceeding through the County Court, where the Court's administrative machinery may not be so quick to achieve a result.

If, of course, there turns out to be a defence and if the claim is for less than £5,000 then the action would normally be transferred to the County Court, which is the proper and cheaper place for litigating over a lesser sum.

Claim rent or forfeit lease?

Why should a landlord choose merely to claim rent when he could pursue the more effective remedy of forfeiture? Two factors which have encouraged landlords to adopt this course have been the recession, which makes properties difficult to re-let, and the fact that general rates, sometimes at a penal level, are levied on empty commercial properties though not (since 1 April 1984) on industrial property. The landlord reasons that if he is unlikely to find a new tenant quickly then, even if he is having a struggle to recover his rent, at least the tenant may pay one day. Also an empty property looks decrepit and is prone to vandalism and fly posting.

The landlord may perhaps conclude that the tenant is financially sound and is merely withholding rent because he has a better use for the money. This must be a matter for his commercial judgment but he may decide that the devil he knows (the existing tenant) is better than the one he does not (some tenant he may happen to find in future).

A third circumstance where the landlord may prefer to exhaust the possibilities of suing his tenant before going for forfeiture is where there is also a personal guarantor. Liability of the guarantor ceases when the lease is finally forfeited, and if the landlord considers that the premises will be difficult to re-let he may prefer to keep the guarantor on the hook for as long as possible. In these circumstances his writ or summons will be against both the tenant and the guarantor.

Finally, as we have already seen, the landlord can always resort to suing the original lessee.

If the landlord is successful in obtaining judgment against his tenant (or guarantor) then the usual array of legal remedies will be open to him. He will now be able to instruct the court bailiffs rather than the certificated bailiffs we mentioned above. If his tenant is a company, the judgment would give him a right to wind it up and he might also be able to obtain a charging order on other premises of the tenant.

Forfeiture

All properly drafted leases contain a 'proviso for forfeiture'. This gives the landlord the right to 're-enter the premises' once the rent is in arrear for a particular period, usually twenty-one days. There are circumstances in which a landlord may choose to re-enter without going to court; for instance, he can instruct a certificated bailiff actually to re-possess the property physically. This can certainly be done where the tenant has clearly abandoned the property, but in view of the possible counter claims by the tenant it is probably prudent in all normal circumstances to effect re-entry using the machinery of the courts. A landlord trying to dispense with action in the court may be liable for damages if he uses undue force; even if he has effected re-entry peaceably, the tenant may claim relief for up to six months after such peaceable re-entry. This is in contrast to the position where the court has ordered forfeiture. (Of course, it must be borne in mind that where the tenancy is residential the landlord has no option but to obtain a court order to recover possession because of the provisions of the Protection from Eviction Act 1977.)

If there is no defence or counter claim for damages, the tenant's only remedy must therefore be to pay the amount claimed into court. If he does not do so the court may still grant relief and give him time to pay. It will very much depend on the particular circumstances of the case.

Plight of subtenant

The position of a subtenant is not an enviable one. If his immediate landlord's lease is forfeited he must apply to the court under section 146(4) of the Law of Property Act 1925 for relief against forfeiture and he must do so before the landlord has resumed possession. He will certainly find himself liable to pay his landlord's arrears and legal costs and to make good any breaches of covenant. Subject to this the court does have discretion to give him relief against forfeiture of his sublease although it is not bound to do so. If he was only occupying part of the premises his liability to meet the landlord's arrears would normally be in proportion to the area occupied by him (*Chatham Empire Theatre (1955) Ltd* v. *Ultrans Ltd* (1961)). It may happen that the subtenant will apply for relief in respect of a period after his sublease has expired. If, but for the forfeiture of the headlease, his lease would have continued under the 1954 Act, then the Court of Appeal has held in the case of *Cadogan* v. *Dimovic* (1984) that the court still has power to make a vesting order in respect of the premises in favour of the subtenant.

All other breaches of covenant

Although to read the average lease you would think that the landlord had precisely the same right of re-entry for other breaches of covenant as he has for non-payment of rent, the fact is that the rules are entirely different because of the operation of section 146 of the Law of Property Act 1925. This section imposes not only special rules in relation to breaches of covenant but also additional rules where the covenant is one of failure to repair.

Section 146 says that before the landlord can enforce the covenants in the lease (other than for non-payment of rent) by action or otherwise he must serve a notice on the tenant:

(a) specifying the breach,
(b) requiring the tenant to remedy the breach (if it is capable of remedy), and
(c) requiring monetary compensation.

The tenant must then have a reasonable time to remedy the breach.

By stating that a notice is needed before re-entry is effected 'by action or otherwise' the section means that, in contrast to the position where rent is in arrear, the landlord cannot peaceably re-enter without first serving a notice. Most leases make the tenant liable for the costs of preparing and serving the notice.

Anyone involved in such procedures should study the section carefully and should prepare the notice with meticulous care. The notice should be served by registered post or recorded delivery. A company should normally be served at its registered office (so a company search should be made immediately before service of the notice). Otherwise service at the premises is normally the correct procedure, although the section refers to the tenant's 'last known place of abode in the United Kingdom'.

How can the tenant rescue himself from this situation? If the breach of covenant is a remediable breach (for instance, a covenant to repair) then complying with the notice will often be sufficient and the landlord will probably never go to court. Some breaches are, however, considered to be irremediable or incapable of remedy; for example, a subletting in breach of covenant. In that case, if the landlord persists the tenant will have to rely on his right to ask the court for relief against forfeiture. If the landlord has commenced legal action the tenant will apply to the same court. If the landlord has served his notice but has not yet issued a writ the tenant may make an application on his own initiative. Again, this can be either to the County Court or to the High Court, depending upon the rateable value of the property. The court has a wide discretion to grant relief. The court's main criterion will be whether the landlord will actually suffer if the tenant is allowed to continue possession of the premises.

As we shall see in Chapter 10, the landlord must take care to ensure that before issue of his writ for forfeiture he does not 'waive' the breach of covenant by accepting rent or behaving in some other way that acknowledges the existence of the tenancy.

Repairing covenants

These are a special category, but in a sense they are the most widely enforced after the covenant for payment of rent.

When a landlord specifies a breach of a repairing covenant he will normally do so in a formal manner, not merely by sending a notice under section 146 but also a schedule of dilapidations, prepared by his surveyors, setting out in detail the work which must be done to remedy the breach. The schedule is, in effect, a specification which must be followed by the tenant's builder in order to comply with the landlord's requirements.

The protection of section 146 alone turned out to be an inadequate protection against unscrupulous landlords and the Leasehold Property (Repairs) Act passed in 1938 gives the tenant additional protection where the lease has more than three years to run. In such cases the landlord's section 146 notice must draw the tenant's attention to his right to serve a counter-notice within twenty-eight days. If the tenant exercises this right and serves the counter-notice, then the landlord must obtain the consent or leave of the court before even starting an action for forfeiture. The court will only give leave if it considers that the value of the landlord's reversion might suffer as a result of the tenant's failure to comply with the schedule.

In practice, surveyors who draw up schedules of dilapidations for commercial properties are well acquainted with this procedure. They know that if they have to prepare a schedule of dilapidations in respect of a property where the lease has more than three years to run, there are many categories of repair (such as minor decorative treatment of the property) which cannot be enforced if the tenant claims the protection of the 1938 Act. What usually happens is that once the section 146 notice and the schedule have been served and the tenant has served his counter-notice, the landlord's and tenant's surveyors get together and pick out those elements in the schedule which it is likely a court would enforce as being items which, if ignored, would damage the landlord's reversion.

Of course, if the tenant refuses to do any works or to co-operate with the landlord's surveyors, the landlord will go to court and hope to obtain leave to commence his forfeiture action on the grounds that his reversion will suffer. A normal action for forfeiture will then follow.

Urgent need for repair

What happens when the need for repair is urgent and the landlord steps in and does the repairs himself? This happened in the case of *Sedac Investments* v. *Tanner* (1982) where masonry was seen to be falling from the roof of the Conservative Association offices in Tonbridge. The landlord, rather than calling on the tenant to do the work, stepped in himself and carried it out. The lease had more than three years to run so the landlord had to obtain the leave of the court to start forfeiture proceedings against the tenant under the provisions of the Leasehold Property (Repairs) Act. The court held that it had no jurisdiction because the works had been carried out before the landlord's application for forfeiture. This rather harsh decision was alleviated in *Hamilton* v. *Martell Securities* (1984) in which the court decided that where the lease gave the landlord an express right of entry to carry out repairs and the landlord exercised this right then he did not need to ask for leave under the 1938 Act but could sue the tenant for the cost of repairs as a debt due under the lease.

Breaches by the landlord

Where the lease is on the usual 'full repairing and insuring terms' the list of landlord's obligations is limited. The occasions when the landlord will be in breach of covenant will accordingly be limited as well. The most usual landlord's covenants will be to grant the tenant 'quiet enjoyment' and to effect insurance, coupled with an obligation to rebuild if an insurance claim is made.

Quiet enjoyment

The covenant to allow the tenant 'quiet enjoyment' would be implied by law if it were not actually set out in the lease, and the courts have to decide as a question of fact whether or not the tenant's 'ordinary and lawful enjoyment of the land is substantially interfered with by the acts of the lessor or those lawfully claiming under him' (*Sanderson* v. *Berwick-upon-Tweed Corporation* (1884)). Mere interference with comfort is not enough, although it might give rise to a claim for nuisance. But an undue amount of noise arising from building works on an adjoining flat has been considered to be a breach of the covenant, as has the construction of scaffolding near to a shop window.

One point the tenant must bear in mind is that if he has an underlease the landlord will not be in breach of the covenant for 'quiet enjoyment' if the superior landlord claims possession. A direct breach will only occur if the immediate landlord has given his subtenant a covenant that his quiet enjoyment will not be interfered with 'by title paramount' which are words the landlord will not readily choose to include in the lease. A subtenant in those circumstances is thrown back on his right to ask the court for relief for forfeiture. (For recent discussion of the point see *Queensway Marketing Ltd* v. *Associated Restaurants Ltd* (1984).)

If a landlord has failed to comply with other covenants, such as direct covenants to repair the building or to effect insurance, then the tenant is in a weaker position because he does not have the leverage of forfeiture to hold over his landlords. He can merely sue for damages or, if circumstances warrant this, try to get an injunction. His main bargaining counter if the landlord has failed to comply with his covenants is to withhold rent. As there is normally no defence to a landlord's claim for non-payment of rent, the tenant must then meet such proceedings by counter-claiming for damages against the landlord for failing to comply with his obligations. This is a ploy which, if successful, can keep the landlord out of his rent for some considerable time unless at an early stage the landlord can prove that the tenant's assertions are without foundation.

Obligations to insure

These days leases which are generally described as 'full repairing and insuring' do not require the tenant to insure the property.

Instead, the landlord must insure the property and the tenant must refund the premiums. The lease will normally place the landlord under an obligation to lay out any insurance monies in rebuilding the property, but in the absence of such a clause the courts will imply such an obligation. Sometimes the lease will indicate that if rebuilding is frustrated the landlord will be at liberty to bring the term to an end and recover his capital loss by retaining the insurance monies. The tenant may nevertheless have a small but proportionate interest in the insurance monies as demonstrated by the case of *Beacon Carpets Ltd* v. *Kirby and Another* (1984) discussed in Chapter 4. As to his other losses, he will it is hoped have remembered to insure the additional risks in connection with his business such as contents, fixtures and loss of profit.

Derogation from grant

As a longstop in the absence of a specific breach of covenant on which to hang his complaint, a tenant may claim that the landlord has 'derogated from his grant'. In essence, this is a common law maxim that having created rights with one hand the landlord must not take them away with the other (*Palmer* v. *Fletcher* (1663)). To be in breach the landlord must act in a way that makes the premises substantially less fit for the purpose for which they were let. For instance, a landlord let premises to a timber merchant and then tried to put up buildings on adjoining land which would have prevented a flow of air to the tenant's timber drying sheds. Because the property had been let for the express purpose of a timber business the court restrained the landlord from acting to the tenant's detriment (*Alding* v. *Latimer Clark Muirhead & Co.* (1894)), but merely letting adjoining property to a competing business is not enough (*Port* v. *Griffith* (1938)). The landlord's activities on land he acquired after the lease was granted will not be derogation, although the tenant has a chance of suing the landlord under his covenant for quiet enjoyment.

Chapter 9

Rent reviews

Before the war and for the first twenty years thereafter a lease of business premises might be granted for a term of seven, fourteen or twenty-one years or more at a fixed rent with no machinery for varying the rent during the term. Inflation has changed all that! In the late 1950s and the 1960s, landlords began to impose rent reviews at successively more frequent intervals as the pace of inflation increased. Nowadays, there will be a review at least every five years and perhaps every three or four depending upon the circumstances and what the market will bear. Paradoxically, five-yearly reviews have become the established norm for prime properties while it is often in leases of poorer properties that reviews tend to crop up at four- or three-yearly intervals.

The legal and surveying professions have been feeling their way throughout this period and the industry of drafting rent review clauses and assessing market rents has now become a highly developed and specialised one. Sometimes there seems to be a tendency to lose sight of the original object of such clauses which is to adjust the rent for monetary inflation and also to take account of changes in the relative value of the property and the surrounding district.

Anyone wishing to delve deeply into the subject must refer to the standard legal textbooks on landlord and tenant or to the specialist reports carried by the *Estates Gazette*, *The Estates Times* or to the *Rent Review Handbook* by Bernstein and Reynolds. My intention in this chapter is to give the practitioner some broad guidance which will help keep him on most of the right lines.

A source of negligence claims

The advent of rent reviews has given rise to many claims for negligence against members of both the legal and surveying professions, and the preparation and service of such notices must be approached with the greatest of care. Most often it is the failure to meet time limits (or the tenant's ability to protect his interests) that has lost the review and has brought about the claim for negligence. Unlike most negligence actions against professional men, the questions to be resolved are not matters of opinion but of objective fact:

(a) Was the surveyor or solicitor responsible for serving the notice?
(b) Did he fail to serve the notice (or the correct notice) within the specified period?
(c) Is service by a specified date 'of the essence'?

If the answer to all three questions is 'yes' then all that remains is for the level of damages to be assessed.

It is particularly in leases drafted in the 60s and early 70s that the draftsman may have created an unintentional pitfall for his clients and their successors. The landlord, the tenant and their respective advisers should look carefully at the relevant clause and ask themselves a number of questions.

Is a 'trigger' notice needed?

Almost all the early rent review clauses (and indeed many of the later ones) indicate that the review cannot be operated until the landlord gives the tenant notice. The lease will often state when the notice must be given (e.g. not more than nine or less than three months before the review date) and also the period of notice (e.g. 'not less than three months' notice'). Many suits for negligence arose (and still arise) because advisers failed to issue the trigger notice in time. A line of cases began to develop to suggest that the landlord who failed to serve his notice in good time must lose his review if the machinery in the lease was akin to an option and he had to serve a notice to invoke it. Fortunately for landlords and their advisers, this view was discredited in *United Scientific Holdings Ltd* v. *Burnley Borough Council* and in *Cheapside Land Development Co. Ltd* v. *Messels Service Co.* (1977).

It is now established that there is a presumption in law *against* time being of the essence in rent review procedures, and this presumption can only be defeated by:

(a) Specific words to the contrary such as 'time shall be of the essence' or 'within three months and not otherwise' (*Drebbond Ltd* v. *Horsham District Council* (1978).
(b) The setting of a strict timetable specifying the alternatives that will occur if a step is not taken.
(c) The construction of the lease as a whole (e.g. where the review occurs at the same time as a tenant's option to break the lease on the review date).
(d) Sufficient surrounding circumstances.
(e) Where one party serves notice on the other that he requires some step to be taken by a specific date and regards time to be of the essence.

Points (c) and (e) were referred to in the obiter dicta (the judges' comments not directly related to the case in hand) in the *United Scientific Holdings* case mentioned above.

Landlords and their advisers must still be on their guard. Quite a number of early rent review clauses do say that time *is* of the essence, either in respect of the 'trigger' notice or of other aspects of the review procedure. For instance, in some leases time is not of the essence to serve the trigger notice but is of the essence for appointing an arbitrator or for asking the President of the RICS to appoint one.

Dangers of the 'deemed' rent notice

Opinion seems to be divided as to whether a trigger notice is desirable in a lease. Many think it is. Moreover, they go on to incorporate the provision that the landlord can insert a proposed rental figure in the notice which, if the tenant does not respond in time by serving a counter-notice, will be binding on the parties. As indicated in Chapter 4, tenants and their advisers should therefore be alert to this possibility in order to avoid the disastrous consequences that might be brought about. For example, a notice might arrive at the registered office of the company or be sent direct to the property, and not be acted upon in time to give the tenant a say as to what the new rent should be. In *Sheridan* v. *Blaircourt Investments Ltd* (1984), there was a time limit during which the tenant had to serve a counter-notice indicating to the landlord that he wished to have the reviewed rent determined by arbitration in default of agreement. The landlord suggested a new increased rent of £40,000, which the tenant considered too high. The landlord's and tenant's agents had discussions and meetings, and correspondence was exchanged in which the tenant *inter alia* indicated that he would like to agree on some other lower figure and that he was mindful of the time limit within which agreement had to be reached and of the alternative option of opting for arbitration on the level of rent. At trial, the judge found that nowhere in the tenant's correspondence was there the necessary *unequivocal* indication to the landlord that he would invoke the arbitration procedure within the time limit allowed. Further, some of the correspondence was headed 'without prejudice and subject to contract' and as such, even if it had been clearer in intention, those words would have prevented the message from being unequivocal. (See too *Shirlcar Properties Ltd* v. *Heinitz* (1983).)

To be valid, notices and counter-notices relating to rent reviews should *not* be marked either 'subject to contract' or 'without prejudice'. This was underlined by the case of *Amalgamated Estates Ltd* v. *Joystretch Manufacturing Ltd* (1980), where the court decided that the rent specified in the notice did not even have to be a bona fide estimate of the market rent. Apparently any figure, however extravagant, would have been binding on the tenant if he failed to object within the stated time limit. The logic of this decision was that time was clearly of the essence and, as the parties had both agreed it, why should the court interfere with a freely negotiated contract?

The opposite course is to draft a review clause which does not need notice at all but simply states that if the review is not agreed by a certain date then it must be referred to an arbitrator or independent expert, as the case may be. If that kind of course applies and the parties are still haggling by the appointed date, then they should enter into a written agreement, perhaps by exchange of letters, stating that they agree to postpone the arbitration date to allow more time for negotiations.

Dilatory landlords

Since the *United Scientific Holdings* case mentioned above was decided, it seems that landlords can be extremely dilatory about operating the rent review procedure and yet be completely successful in establishing a review from the original date and collecting not only the increased rent from that date but also interest! Although you might think landlords would be anxious to establish their new rent as quickly as possible, they and their surveyors sometimes form the view that it would be better to wait and see what 'comparables' emerge in other buildings in the locality, in the hope that the longer they wait the more favourable this will be to the landlord's interests.

The courts seem to have been very benevolent to dilatory landlords. The only criterion seems to be whether the late enforcement of the review has a detrimental effect on the tenant's interest and, almost always, they have considered it is not the case and the landlord has got his review. In *Amherst* v. *James Walker Goldsmith & Silversmith Ltd* (1983) a twenty-eight year lease was granted in 1961 at a rent of £2500 p.a. and the review, which fell due in 1975, required notice to be given by 24 December 1974. Time was not of the essence. For various reasons the landlord's notice, requiring the rent to be increased to £16,000 per annum was not served until 1979. A similar case was *London & Manchester Assurance Co. Ltd* v. *G.A. Dunn & Co.* (1981) where a notice which could have been served in 1976 was delayed until 1980. This was still valid. There had to be some factor other than mere delay to allow the tenant to defeat a late review notice.

There were, however, some special circumstances in both the above cases. In the *Amherst* case the delay had occurred because of earlier litigation on the question of whether time *was* of the essence for service of a trigger notice, and after that litigation was successful. The 1983 case arose over whether the delay in applying to the RICS was sufficient to make time of the essence. In the *London & Manchester* case the delay occurred because the landlord believed the review had been lost, and the period between the original date and the *United Scientific Holdings* decision had to be disregarded in considering whether unreasonable delay had occurred.

Where a notice has been missed and where time is not of the essence, a landlord or a tenant may still lose his rights if any action on his part causes the other party to believe that he has abandoned his right to the review. On the other hand, even where time is of the essence and notice is missed, the landlord or tenant may still retain his rights if the other party led him to believe that he did not regard time as being of the essence. It may also be possible to obtain relief where the delay relates to the appointment of an arbitrator under the provisions of the Arbitration Act 1950.

Strict time limit applies to all stages of review

If time is stated in the lease to be of the essence, the parties can not relax once the original trigger notice is served in good time. The time clause normally extends to all stages of the review.

In the *Amherst* case, the review clause in the lease not only specified a date for serving the landlord's notice but also provided for agreement on the new rent to be reached by another specified date, after which the rent had to be determined by a surveyor appointed by the RICS. However, the lease did not specify the last date by which the approach to the RICS had to be made so the court held that a late application to have a surveyor appointed *was* valid as time could not be of the essence regarding that application. In *Essoldo Ltd* v. *Elcresta Ltd* (1971) it was held that an application to the RICS would not be invalidated solely on the grounds that there had been no attempt to agree a rent.

Rental values

You might think that it would be a simple enough matter to decide what the market rent for a building should be, but you would be falling into the same trap as the early rent review clause draftsmen. Rental values have to be very closely defined before a valuer who has been asked to advise upon or determine a rent review can give an answer. Differing definitions of the 'market rent' can substantially affect his advice. Among the factors that may have a significant bearing on the rental value are the following:

(a) What does vacant possession mean? If there are many sub-tenants it can be crucial to know if the sublet parts of the property are vacant as well (*99 Bishopsgate Ltd* v. *Prudential Assurance Co. Ltd* (1984)).
(b) Do you assume a willing tenant? In *F.R. Evans (Leeds) Ltd* v. *English Electric Co. Ltd* (1977) the effect of the meaning of those words was a difference of £285,000. The market rent would be £290,000 without a willing tenant and £515,000 with a willing tenant!
(c) What term is to be valued? The original term or the term unexpired at review which may be so short as to affect the rental?

(d) What matters are to be disregarded? Tenant's occupation of the property itself? Tenant's occupation of adjacent property? Tenant's improvements? Tenant's goodwill? Rent control of residential upper part? Specific lease restrictions on permitted use? Is the valuer required to disregard a particular clause of the lease, such as the rent review clause itself?

(e) If one were marketing the hypothetical lease, would there be any terms which would affect its marketability and hence its value?

(f) Are there any artificial assumptions? For example, are you supposed to value the premises as offices even though they are actually used as an hotel?

Restrictive user clause: effect on rent

As an example of the specialist surveyor's art, let us look at the 'user restriction clause' argument. Often properties are marketed on the basis that when a tenant is found, the lease he receives will restrict him to using the property for his own particular trade. However, when the rent review arrives the valuer is asked to *assume* that the property would be marketed on the basis that the *only* permitted use is the trade carried on by the present tenant. It would be more realistic to tell the valuer to assume that the property would be let to the highest bidder who would *then* be required to sign a lease restricting use to *his* particular trade.

How much a restrictive user clause will affect the reviewed rent will depend partly on the obscurity of the use restriction and partly on the relative prosperity of the permitted trade or business at the time of review. Just because a bone boiler was the highest bidder in 1954 does not mean to say he will be the highest bidder today. In *Plinth Property Investments Ltd* v. *Mott Hay & Anderson* (1978) it was agreed before the hearing that if the user argument stated above was correct (and the court said it was), the difference made the market rent on a restricted basis 31.6 per cent lower than the market rent assessed on an unrestricted basis.

Need to reinstate does not reduce rent

An attempt by the proprietor of a dolphinarium to argue that his obligation to put the property back into its original state meant that his rent on review should be reduced, was unsuccessful. In *Pleasurama Properties Ltd* v. *Leisure Investments (West End) Ltd* (1984) the tenant pointed out that the licence which permitted the change from a retail use and associated works contained an obligation to reinstate at the end of the term. He argued that the cost of such reinstatement works should be taken into account when fixing the new rent. The High Court rejected this contention. The landlord had received no additional rent or other benefit by issuing his consent. Mr Justice Nourse found no evidence that the parties intended that the landlord should suffer for requiring the premises to be reinstated.

Artificial assumptions

As we have seen, if the lease is worded so as to impose certain assumptions on the parties (even if they are quite unrealistic) the courts will not enquire whether or not they are fair but will enforce the bargain the parties made. How far the 'assumptions' on which the review is deemed to take place will have any bearing on the ultimate rent will differ according to the particular circumstances. Sometimes their effects may be very marginal, and can therefore be ignored. Sometimes, as in the case of deemed office use, they can be quite substantial.

In *Bovis Group Pension Fund Ltd* v. *GC Flooring & Furnishing* (1982) the rent of a building was to be reviewed on the assumption that the whole could be let for office purposes. The arbitrator appointed to fix the rent considered that it had a value of £85,000 per annum on that assumption. In fact, however, only two out of the five floors had a permitted use for office purposes under the Planning Acts. The arbitrator found that if the rent were to be fixed on this more realistic basis it would be reduced to £75,000 per annum. The court held that the artificial assumptions in the lease prevailed over reality and that the correct rent was £85,000 per annum.

Where rent reviews are at long intervals, such as twenty-one years, this will affect the market value. Clearly, a tenant will pay a greater rent fixed for twenty-one years than he would pay on a modern lease with five-yearly reviews. Some leases have been granted with five-yearly review clauses where the rent on review has to be assessed as if there were no review at all. The court will uphold this fiction although the results may be horrific for the tenant (*Pugh* v. *Smiths Industries Ltd* (1982)).

Artificial assumptions can, however, 'bite back' when the time comes to renew the lease under the Landlord and Tenant Act 1954. Under section 34 of that Act the rent the court determines must reflect the terms of the renewed lease. If the court orders that the same rent review clause must reappear in the new lease (and it has not yet been established if the court will necessarily do this), then the artificial nature of the review clause could well depress the rent the court will order.

The best advice to tenants is to look before you leap, but if you do find yourself with a lease of this nature you will discover that the courts will uphold the landlord's right to impose a rent which is greater than what you would pay as the fair market rent for your premises.

Beware of the minefield

From this brief outline it will be noted that the rent review clause is a minefield for the unwary. The main difficulty is that, although many of the traps are known to the specialist solicitors and surveyors who practise in this field, there are still many others that have not been tested in the courts and, no doubt, many more that have yet to be discovered. There has been an explosion of litigation on the subject over the last fifteen years and the sophistication of the arguments put forward by specialist valuers, solicitors and counsel suggest that there will be many more cases in the future.

To those advising their hapless clients on the subject, the best advice can only be to keep fully up to date on the subject (or to take specialist advice from someone who is).

It is also essential that the various advisers whom the client has retained to advise him communicate with one another. Many of the blunders seen in existing review clauses (even modern ones) could have been avoided if, for instance, the solicitor drafting or approving the clause had asked his client's surveyor, 'What do you think the clause means?' The solicitor should make tactful enquiries to ensure that the surveyor to whom he addresses this question is someone familiar with the legal and technical aspects of rent reviews; preferably someone who encounters the subject on a daily basis. The surveyor or negotiator who secured the property for the tenant may be brilliant at marketing but a novice where rent reviews are concerned. If he is a member of a large firm it may have a specialist department to advise on such matters. As in the medical field, the best general practitioner is the one who knows when to call in a specialist.

Finding the expert or arbitrator

The lease will normally lay down machinery for appointing someone to determine the rent if the parties fail to agree. Often, if they have been unable to agree on the rent, they still have a chance to agree on the appointment of an expert or arbitrator; but if they have not been able to agree that either then it is usually the President of the Royal Institution of Chartered Surveyors who is asked to make the nomination.

The RICS has an arbitration department which handles the administrative side of the appointment for a fee (currently £60 plus VAT), but it can take some time. If by some omission the lease does not have any machinery for getting someone to fix the rent once negotiations have broken down, it was once thought that the court would not interfere. However, a case in the House of Lords (*Sudbrook Trading Estate* v. *Eggleton* (1982)) indicated that the court might imply the missing terms in order to see that the bargain originally envisaged by the parties would be implemented. That was a case about the exercise of an option to purchase the freehold, but it seems quite likely that the same would apply to a rent review clause which was defective in this respect.

Opinion also seems divided on whether it is better for the review clause to specify that the rent should be determined by an expert rather than an arbitrator. From the viewpoint of the parties, the practical difference is that an expert is required to make his own decision whereas an arbitrator acts on the basis of submissions from the parties. There is also a distinction as to the degree of finality between the expert's determination on the one hand and an arbitration on the other.

The need for submissions by the parties

Here the differences may not be so great as they appear, because although an expert may be appointed and told to get on with it he will almost always invite the parties to submit evidence to assist him in reaching his decision. He is, however, entitled to go round the district making his own enquiries, and from his own knowledge to determine what the new rent should be.

An arbitrator must act in a judicial capacity and is therefore bound to allow the parties to be heard. An arbitration is governed by the provisions of the Arbitration Acts 1950 and 1979, and the legislation and surrounding case law has created an entire body of law to assist the parties. The Acts cover many procedural points; for example, on how to remove or replace the arbitrator, controlling disputes, giving access to the courts to enable discovery of documents to be ordered, rules on the admissability of evidence, costs, rights of appeal determining points of law and so forth.

Appeals

On the question of the right to appeal, if the parties have agreed to accept the determination of an expert valuer (as opposed to an arbitrator) then it seems that a 'non speaking valuation of the right property by the right man' can not be impugned (*Burgess* v. *Purchase & Sons (Farms) Ltd* (1983)). The same case indicates that a 'speaking award' (by an expert who sets out his reasons) *can* be impugned if it is clear that the award was made on a fundamentally erroneous basis and was not what the parties contracted for. Thus the only means of attacking the award of an expert is an action for negligence: the remedy would be damages, not the setting aside of his decision.

An arbitrator is acting in a semi-judicial capacity and he cannot be sued for negligence. Since the Arbitration Act 1979, an appeal on a point of law can still be made, but only if the point in issue could 'substantially affect the rights of the parties'. An example occurred in *Segama NV* v. *Penny le Roy Ltd* (1983). There, the judge considered whether there could be an appeal on two questions; if rents of comparable properties agreed after the actual review date were admissible as evidence of the new rent, and if rents concluded with existing tenants (as opposed to lettings of vacant properties) were admissible as evidence. The judge agreed with the arbitrator in this particular case that both types of comparables were admissible. He conceded, however, that both matters were points of law of some public importance. Nevertheless, not only had the landlord not made out a strong prima facie case that the arbitration was wrong but the practical effect of the rent (£1000 per annum over five years) was not great enough 'to substantially affect the rights of one or more of the parties'.

Avoid sloppy drafting

It is of course desirable that the lease should be properly drafted, avoiding loosely worded references to 'arbitration by an expert'. The parties should be seen to make a clear choice of the manner in which a disputed rent review is to be settled. The lease must say that the dispute must be referred to arbitration, or alternatively that reference is to be to a surveyor acting as an *expert*. The use of the expression 'independent surveyor' causes problems. It has been held that the word 'independent' means he is to be neither the landlord's nor the tenant's surveyor but does not imply that he should act 'independently'.

If the rent review clause says that 'in the event of a dispute' the rent is to be determined 'by an independent surveyor appointed jointly by the parties' and that his decision is to be final and binding upon them, it has been held that he should act as an arbitrator. However, the lease may have a separate clause requiring the parties to submit other kinds of disputes to arbitration and if this is the case the presumption that the review clause requires the surveyor to act like an arbitrator will be defeated.

Expert or arbitrator?

I do not propose to recommend that either one course or the other is the correct one. It would depend on the parties and what they conceive to be their respective interests. Determination of rent by an expert is probably quicker and less troublesome but, particularly if he does not explain his decision, he is likely to have an aggrieved party without redress. An arbitration ensures that the parties may have their say but, unless a point of law is at stake, the arbitrator's findings can not be attacked. Where the property is of a special nature with little likelihood of comparable evidence of value it is more appropriate to call for the appointment of an expert. An arbitrator, by the very nature of his appointment, must reach his decision on the basis of the evidence before him. For a case illustrating this, see *Top Shop Estates Ltd* v. *Tandy Ltd* (1985). The court set aside the ruling of an arbitrator who, without referring to the parties, and on his own initiative, arranged a 'head count' to help him assess the volume of passing trade.

It is to course usual to decide on the question of expert or arbitrator during the drafting of the lease. Nevertheless, after the dispute arises there is nothing to stop the parties changing their minds, and so long as they record their agreement to the change they can, for instance, require the expert to hear or receive submissions.

In practice, in the vast majority of cases the determination of the rent either by an expert or by an arbitrator is accepted by the parties. It is, of course, only those which are not accepted which come to the notice of the courts.

Costs

Leases usually provide that the costs of the reference to an expert are to be shared by the parties or that they should be in the award of the expert. In contrast, where an arbitrator is called for, an agreement made prior to the dispute that one or both parties should meet the costs of the operation is void (Arbitration Act 1950, section 18(3)). Moreover, the arbitrator has the power not merely to order a party to pay his (the arbitrator's) costs, but also those of the other side to the dispute. There is therefore a danger that a spurious reference to arbitration will result in the person initiating the reference having to pay the other side's costs. If there is a dispute over the level of the costs themselves the point, in an arbitration, can be referred to a High Court Taxing Master, as can the costs in any High Court litigation.

Chapter 10

End of term

The tenancy originally created by a lease or tenancy agreement can come to an end in a variety of ways, and the date specified in writing may well not be the date upon which it ends. It can terminate early because the landlord has forfeited or re-entered and it can also end early because the parties have agreed that it should be surrendered. It can just run out and the tenant can leave. Or usually these days it can run on with the protection which occupying business tenants enjoy under the Landlord and Tenant Act 1954. Let us consider the possibilities in turn.

Premature termination by forfeiture

We have already seen that the landlord's major sanction against breaches of covenant including non-payment of rent by the tenant is forfeiture of the lease. Most leases contain a proviso that the landlord is entitled to do this if rent is unpaid for fourteen or twenty-one days or if the tenant is in breach of covenant. As we have already seen, except where the breach of covenant is non-payment of rent the landlord must first follow the procedure laid down by section 146 of the Law of Property Act 1925, namely the service of the prescribed form of notice. Under the same section the tenant has a right to claim relief from the court even if the breach is proved. But ultimately, if the landlord has proved his case and the court has refused to grant relief to the tenant, the court will order forfeiture and the lease will come to an end. In some circumstances the tenant may, in addition, be liable to the landlord for damages.

The effect of the forfeiture is to terminate the legal estate formerly held by the tenant so that it is extinguished, and the reversion (usually the freehold) will then be free of it and the landlord will be entitled to re-let. If proceedings are initiated for forfeiture of a lease the landlord's solicitors should be sure to have these proceedings registered as a Land Charge (a 'pending action') as notice to anyone proposing to take over the lease that the proceedings are in hand. Otherwise the tenant might be able to divest himself of the lease to an innocent purchaser and avoid the rigours of the proceedings. Without such registration the purchaser will not be bound by the pending action unless he has had express notice of it.

Waiver: how the landlord can lose right to forfeit

The issue of a writ is an irrevocable sign by the landlord that he has chosen to forfeit the lease. Until then the landlord can lose his right to forfeit by waiving his rights. It is for the tenant to prove that, knowing of the breach of covenant, the landlord performed some act which recognised that the relationship of landlord and tenant was continuing.

The most obvious of such acts is to accept rent. This applies even if the landlord demanded the rent as a result of a clerical error on the part of his agents (*Central Estates (Belgravia) Ltd* v. *Woolgar* (1972)). However, if the landlord realises his mistake and withdraws the demand before it has been communicated to the tenant then he has not waived the breach of covenant (*Henry Smith Charity Trustees* v. *Willson* (1983)), nor is the breach waived if the landlord simply stands by and takes no action, e.g. by allowing the tenant to go ahead and carry out alterations without having first obtained consent.

In addition, some breaches of covenant are regarded as 'continuing breaches' even if the landlord has accepted rent. This applies in particular to breaches of repairing covenants.

The 'twilight period'

The Court of Appeal considered at some length in the case of *Associated Deliveries Ltd* v. *Harrison and Prichard* (1984) what was described as a 'twilight period' between the time that a writ for forfeiture had been issued and forfeiture actually taking place. The premises had been vandalised between the relevant dates. Because, as already noted, forfeiture is an irrevocable step by the landlord denying the lease and the tenant's covenants under it, it was clear that the landlord could not sue the tenant for a breach of his repairing covenant arising from these acts of vandalism. That is why tenants are sued for 'mesne profits' and not for rent once forfeiture has been initiated. In this case the Court of Appeal indicated that the tenant might be liable in tort. Solicitors and counsel drafting pleadings in cases of this kind must be careful to settle these pleadings correctly. It is not sufficient for them to rely on the covenants in the lease as these covenants are already at an end once the forfeiture has commenced.

Once the lease has come to an end, the landlord's solicitors will be prudent to place a copy of the court order among the deeds to make it clear to anyone inspecting the documents that, although it was a lease which had apparently several more years left to run, it is now at an end. Where the lease is affected by Land Registration Acts, i.e. being more than twenty-one years in length with notice against the landlord's title or registered in its own right, then steps should be taken to close the register and get rid of the entry of the lease on the landlord's title.

Peaceable re-entry

There will be some circumstances in which the landlord may be able to take the wording of the lease literally, peaceably re-enter the property and treat the lease as terminated. In securing entry he must not break the criminal law by threatening violence against a person or property (Criminal Law Act 1977, section 6), and of course the tenancy must not be a residential one protected by the Rent Acts. Force may not be used even if the occupiers are squatters but, once having regained possession, the landlord is entitled to maintain his possession forcibly. In any event he will probably change the locks.

In the case of premises where there are subtenants the landlord may not mind their continued occupation so long as he gets the rent they have formerly been paying to their immediate landlord. In such a case he would exercise his right of re-entry by posting a notice stating that he is now their landlord and that future rents are payable to him. He needs to be pretty sure of his ground to avoid a claim for damages by his tenant, but in selected circumstances he may be entitled to do this. The disadvantage is the lack of documentary proof that the legal term has terminated. Perhaps a statutory declaration by the landlord or his agent should be posted with the deeds explaining what has happened.

Abandoned premises

It may happen that a tenant who fails to pay rent for a considerable time abandons the premises, encouraging the landlord to feel that he may treat them as his own once more. The landlord should take positive steps to assert his re-entry by changing the locks and posting notices to the property.

Where the tenant has left the property and the landlord is in the position of being entitled to serve a notice to quit (as in the case of monthly or quarterly tenancy) the Landlord and Tenant Act 1954 provides a procedure (section 54) allowing the landlord to ask the County Court to order the determination of the tenancy. The landlord has to satisfy the court that he has taken all reasonable steps to contact the tenant and that no rent has been paid during the six months prior to his application.

There is an analogous procedure for recovering deserted premises by applying to the Magistrates' Court under the Distress for Rent Act 1737. Again, half a year's rent must be in arrear. The landlord can ask the magistrates to view the premises. They will fix a notice on the property advising the tenant that they will attend again in not less than fourteen days. If the tenant has still failed to appear the justices have a right to declare the remainder of the lease void. This right is still on the statute books but there seems to be no recent case law on the subject.

The need to use these two procedures is minimised by the fact that leases contain provisions that notices are effective if sent to the premises or the tenant's last known address.

Premature determination by surrender

The landlord and the tenant may reach a mutual agreement to bring the lease to a premature end enabling the tenant to surrender his lease. This can be done in a formal manner by a contract (see below) and subsequently a deed of surrender, or it can be done by operation of law which means that the tenant gives up possession of the premises, handing over the keys of the premises and usually his lease as well. This is a perfectly valid way of bringing the tenancy to an end so long as it is with the landlord's agreement. In contrast is the position of the liquidator or the trustee in bankruptcy of an insolvent tenant. He has the power, within twelve months of his appointment, to disclaim the lease by written notice to the landlord and this has the effect of terminating the lease. Any underlease will survive but only if the subtenant fulfils the obligations of the headlease. In such circumstances he can ask for the bankrupt tenant's lease to be vested in him.

Surrender by operation of law also, incidentally, takes place if the landlord grants the tenant a new lease before his old one has expired. In that case the old one is treated as surrendered in the same manner.

Agreement to surrender business premises may not be valid

In this book we are dealing with business premises, and because the renewal provisions of the Landlord and Tenant Act 1954 can only be avoided with the sanction of the court, a written agreement for a future surrender will not normally be valid unless an order of the court has been obtained.

In *Tarjomani* v. *Panther Securities Ltd* (1982) the tenant of a shop fell into arrears with his rent. He signed a letter offering to surrender his lease immediately and to give up the premises twenty-eight days later in return for the landlord releasing him from the arrears. He then refused to move out and the court agreed that as the surrender did not take immediate effect it was an agreement to do so at a later date, and as such it was unenforceable because of the restrictions on contracting out of the 1954 Act. However, if the parties go straight to completion without an intervening contract the surrender itself will be perfectly valid.

Releasing the tenant

A tenant who is about to surrender his lease will want to know that having done so he will not be under any outstanding liability. It is not an implied term of the surrender that he is released from his obligations and it is therefore sensible, particularly if there is any doubt over the matter, that he should obtain an express release from the landlord. In such circumstances a written surrender is desirable. It should be noted that underleases survive the surrender of the immediate landlord's lease. The reversioner accepts the surrender subject to any subsisting subtenancies. If there is a rent review pending at the time the lease is surrendered but the figure is only fixed by the arbitrator some time later, the guarantors of the lease may find themselves liable to meet the extra rent up to the date of surrender (*Torminster* v. *Green* (1983)), so it would seem prudent for a deed of surrender to include releases of the guarantors as well as of the tenants themselves.

Premature determination by merger

Another way a lease can come to an end before its due date is where the tenant himself has become the landlord and the two separately-held interests merge. In some cases the parties will not want the leasehold and freehold to merge. For instance, the tenant acquiring the freehold may subsequently wish to assign the lease separately or he may wish to mortgage them to different people or leave one interest mortgaged and the other free from incumbrances. The courts will normally treat the two interests as merged unless there is clear evidence that the tenant's intention was that the merger should not take place.

Distinction between forfeiture and voluntary surrender or merger

The important practical difference between voluntary acts bringing the lease to an end (such as surrender or merger) and termination as a result of forfeiture or re-entry is that the surrender or merger of leases leaves intact any underlease that the tenant may have created. For instance, where the freeholder has a tenant who in turn has several subtenants and the tenant surrenders his lease, the subtenants become the direct tenants of the landlord and pay their rent to him.

However, where the lease is forfeited either by order of the court or by peaceable re-entry the undertenants are in a perilous position and must claim relief from forfeiture under section 146(4) of the Law of Property Act 1925. This allows the court to order that the subtenants should be treated as the direct tenants of the landlord but on such terms as to rent, costs and damages as the court may think fit. Clearly the subtenant could end up paying a great deal more and be subject to terms more severe than those prescribed by the underlease itself. The subtenant's mortgagee, incidentally, also has similar rights.

Termination as a result of compulsory purchase

We tend to think of compulsory purchase as something affecting freehold land but of course compulsory acquisition of leasehold interests can readily occur. Leases from year to year or for shorter periods are treated in a special manner, but longer tenancies are treated in the same way as freeholds.

Once a compulsory purchase order has been made a Notice to Treat must be served on the leaseholder under the Acquisition of Land Act 1981. A Notice to Treat is, in effect, a contract for sale and purchase but it is not enforceable until the purchase price has been fixed. Anyone who takes over the lease by assignment will take it subject to the Notice to Treat, whether or not he has actual notice of it. The amount of compensation, if not agreed, has to be determined by the Lands Tribunal. The basis of compensation is open market value.

Of course the lease may not be a very long one and the authority, having acquired the freehold interest, may be content to await the expiry of the lease and terminate it in the usual way by the service of a notice under section 25 of the 1954 Landlord and Tenant Act (see below). In such a case the tenant would be entitled to the same statutory compensation as if the landlord had terminated his tenancy. In the case of 'minor tenancies' (those from year to year or less) the Notice to Treat is not required. Compensation for such tenancies is assessed on the assumption that the tenant would have had a right to apply for a new tenancy if it were not for the compulsory purchase. If, however, the statutory compensation would be greater, the tenant will receive this.

When the lease ends on the prescribed date

When a lease stops on the agreed date it is said to 'expire by effluxion of time'. Due to the protection afforded to business tenants by the Landlord and Tenant Act 1954 it will hardly ever occur in the case of commercial leases. This observation applies with equal force to a lease brought to an end by the landlord invoking a break clause or rebuilding clause. A notice implementing such a clause will bring forward the date that the 'common law' tenancy expires, but it will not avoid the need for the landlord to serve the proper notices under section 25 of the 1954 Act in which he must, if appropriate, specify the grounds on which he proposes to resist a new tenancy.

Of course, if a tenant under the lease is no longer occupying any part of the premises he will not be entitled to the protection of the 1954 Act. If, for instance, he has moved out with no intention to return or if he has sublet the whole of the premises he will not qualify. In those cases his lease will simply run out. The only other circumstances in which the lease of premises of a commercial tenant will fail to continue is where the parties have taken the special action required under the amendments created by the Law of Property Act 1969. These allow the parties to contract out of the 1954 Act with the agreement of the court. Where this procedure has been correctly adopted the lease will come to an end on its specified date and the tenant's rights of occupation will cease.

There will be many occasions when the tenant knows in advance that he does not want a new tenancy. Strictly speaking, a business tenant in this position should give his landlord notice of his intention not less than three months before the date that the lease is due to expire. This same procedure applies if the lease is continuing under the provision of the 1954 Act, although different procedures will apply once notices have been served and applications made under the Act.

Inadvertently creating a new tenancy

Landlords and their agents should be particularly careful to ensure that where the lease is due to come to an end they do not, by mistake, demand or accept a further quarter's rent from the tenant. If they do and the rent is paid, this could set up a new 'periodic' tenancy.

Take the following example. A lease is due to expire on 24 December 1985. The tenant has sublet the whole property and so does not have the protection of the 1954 Act. Nevertheless, during

December 1985 the landlord inadvertently posts a rent demand to the tenant for the rent due in advance for the three-month period from 25 December 1985. The tenant pays it. This creates a three-monthly or quarterly tenancy at common law which can only be brought to an end by the service of three months' notice to expire at the end of the rent period. So the earliest date by which the landlord can terminate the new tenancy he has created is 24 June 1986, and to do so he must serve his notice by 24 March 1986.

This example relates to a tenancy expiring at common law to which the rules laid down by the Landlord and Tenant Act 1954 do not apply. In the next chapter we will look at the way that Act governs the termination of business tenancies.

Chapter 11

Termination and renewal of leases under the 1954 Act

The scheme of protection of the 1954 Act

The essence of the Act is that where premises are occupied by the tenant for the purposes of his own business his tenancy does not come to an end but continues unless the special notices described by the Act have been served. Printed forms are available from law stationers. Care should be taken not to use out of date forms, as they do change from time to time. If the forms are copied the notes on the back must be copied too.

It is usually the landlord who will initiate the process by serving a section 25 notice. For the time being, let us assume that we are dealing with a tenant in occupation of the whole of the premises. The notice must expire after the correct statutory period. The landlord will normally be looking forward to an increased rent and, therefore, will want to bring the tenancy legally to an end at the earliest opportunity, namely the date on which the lease formally comes to an end. The rule is that the notice must be served between six and twelve months before the date specified in the notice as the termination date. That date in turn must be no earlier than the date upon which the tenancy would end at common law. This will normally mean the date specified at the end of the lease, but if the landlord has inadvertently allowed the tenancy to run on (as in the example given in the previous chapter) then the notice must be of at least six months.

For example, a lease expires on 24 December 1984. The landlord can therefore serve his section 25 notice any time after 25 December 1983, but because a minimum of six clear months notice must be given he must try to serve the notice not later than 24 June. If he forgets to do so until July, he will have to specify a termination date at the end of January to ensure that the tenant has received six clear months' notice.

Prepare the notice with care

The landlord or his advisers should prepare the notice with care to ensure that it is not invalid. The tenant's name must be correctly given and the property occupied by the tenant ('the holding') correctly described. The notice must be properly served: on the registered office if the tenant is a company, and normally on the premises themselves if the tenant is an individual or a partnership.

In this notice the landlord must state whether or not he intends to oppose the grant of a new tenancy. If he does not mind the grant of a new lease he will leave in the printed words on the section 25 notice which state that the landlord 'does not oppose the grant of a new tenancy'.

The landlord must leave no doubt in the mind of the tenant as to whether or not an application to the court for a new lease will be opposed. He should not add any conditions to the form on this point. If the landlord feels that he may wish to oppose the tenant's application he must be careful to select *all* the relevant grounds for his refusal at this stage. Grounds for opposing the new tenancy can not be added at a later stage, although they may be deleted.

The tenant's alternative

The 1954 Act provides an alternative route to termination and renewal of the lease. It allows the tenant to take the initiative by serving a tenant's request for a new tenancy under section 26. He can not do this if the landlord has already served a section 25 notice. Equally, once the tenant has served his request the landlord cannot serve a section 25 notice.

In his notice the tenant asks for a new tenancy starting not less than six and not more than twelve months from the date of his notice, the date in question being once more not earlier than the earliest date that the tenancy could have come to an end at common law. Since the effect of his request is to bring his own tenancy to an end on that date, why should the tenant initiate the process in this way?

Firstly, the tenant may be keen to settle matters for the future. Although he could just wait for the landlord's notice he might have compelling business reasons for wanting to know what the future will hold. Secondly, he can turn delay by the landlord to his advantage by the so-called 'leap-frogging technique'. In his notice he can ask for the present tenancy to end and the new tenancy to begin in between six and twelve months' time. Clearly the tenant would like to put off paying more rent for as long as possible so he will ask for his new lease to start in twelve months. It is like a game of cat and mouse. For example, the lease ends on 25 December 1985. The landlord could have served a section 25 notice any time after 25 December 1984 but by June 1985 he has still not done so. The tenant then serves a tenant's request for a new tenancy commencing on 1 June 1986, i.e. twelve months' time. He now remains at the property at the old rent for an extra five and a half months. Of course, if the landlord had managed to serve his notice during May he would have specified 25 December 1985 as the date for the landlord to end and the tenant would lose any advantage. For the tenant it is a matter of guesswork and nerve, but for the landlord the moral is clear: serve your section 25 notice as early as possible in the last year of the term.

When a tenant's request is served, the landlord must decide whether he intends to exercise his right to oppose the grant of a new lease. He has two months to serve a counter-notice stating the grounds upon which he will oppose the new tenancy.

Grounds of opposition

In his notice (either his own notice under section 25 or his counter-notice to the tenant's section 26 request) the landlord must choose whether he is proposing to oppose the grant of a new lease. He is entitled to do so on one of the grounds which are specified under section 30 of the 1954 Act and which are set out on the reverse of the printed form. The wording should be studied with care but, stated simply, the grounds are:

(a) that the tenant has not kept the property repaired in accordance with his obligations;
(b) that he has persistently delayed paying rent;
(c) that he has been in breach of the covenants in the lease;
(d) that the landlord has offered him reasonable alternative accommodation suitable to his requirements;
(e) that, if the tenant is merely a subtenant of part of the property, the landlord considers he could let the whole of the property at a greater rent;

(f) that the landlord intends to demolish or re-construct the premises and could not reasonably do so if the tenant remains in possession; and

(g) that the landlord intends to occupy the tenant's premises either for the purposes of a business to be carried on by him or as his own residence.

The landlord should not be frivolous in seeking to oppose a new tenancy because the grounds for his opposition will be put to the test by the court, assuming the matter goes that far. He should also bear in mind that if the grounds on which he opposes are not due to the tenant's behaviour ((a), (b) or (c) above) but are due to the landlord's own requirements ((e), (f) and (g)), the tenant will be entitled to compensation based on the rateable value of the property. (Currently this is 3 times the rateable value if the tenant has been in occupation for more than fourteen years and 6 times the rateable value if his period of occupation, which includes that of predecessors in his business, exceeds fourteen years. See also below.)

Tenant must serve a counter-notice or lose his rights

Every tenant must be aware that once the landlord's termination notice under section 25 has been served he has only two months in which to serve a counter-notice. If he wants the protection of the 1954 Act he must give the landlord written notice not later than two months after the section 25 notice was served on him to the effect that he does not intend to give up possession of the premises. There is a printed form of this notice but a valid notice can be given informally so long as it is in writing. A suitably worded letter will do, if it clearly states that the tenant does not intend to give up possession.

Serving the counter-notice is not in itself sufficient to preserve the tenant's rights. It gets him over the first hurdle by preserving his right to apply to the court, but he must also exercise *that* right within strict time limits; namely between two and four months from the date of service of the landlord's notice (*not*, it should be noted, from the date of the counter-notice). The tenant's right to ask the court for a new tenancy will therefore be lost unless the application itself has been lodged in good time. Moreover, if it was the tenant who took the initiative by making a tenant's request the two to four months' time limit applies from the time he served his notice *whether or not* the landlord bothered to serve the counter-notice, so in neither case can the tenant sit back. He must put his application forward within the two to four month period.

High Court or County Court?

In the vast majority of cases the application is made to the County Court. The High Court is involved when the 'holding' has a rateable value exceeding a prescribed limit, at present £5000. Therefore the application relating to the average high street shop or small suite of offices will almost certainly be to a County Court but if the holding comprises a supermarket or a block of offices or possibly a large shop in a 'prime' position then the High Court is likely to be involved.

There are minor differences between the proceedings in the courts but essentially the course of both kinds of application runs on similar lines. If there is some doubt as to the rateable value (perhaps because the tenant's premises are not separately rated), machinery exists under the Landlord and Tenant (Determination of Rateable Value Procedure) Rules 1954 for the matter to be referred to the Commissioners for Inland Revenue, acting on the advice of a valuation officer with a right of appeal to the Lands Tribunal.

Time to negotiate

It should be noted that the tenant is not at liberty to make his application to the court until two months have elapsed since the service of the landlord's notice. Parliament's intention in setting this time limit was to give the parties time to negotiate. Sometimes this will work out well and the landlord and tenant will reach agreement on all the terms for renewal of the lease, if not within the first couple of months then at least before the four-month period for application to the court has expired.

If terms for a new lease are agreed in principle during this period it is important, particularly for the tenant, to remember that if the negotiations have been 'subject to contract' his new tenancy will not necessarily be secure. Either a binding lease or a valid agreement for a lease would be necessary.

At the very least the tenant must be sure that the landlord has recorded his proposals in open correspondence which the tenant can turn into a binding contract by signifying in writing his unconditional acceptance of the terms. If there is even a scintilla of doubt as to whether the landlord is bound to grant a new lease, it is always advisable to put in the application to the court. It is not a complex or expensive matter (the County Court fee is £15 at present) and is well worth while to ensure that the tenant is not left vulnerable to a last minute renegotiation with the landlord holding all the cards.

The 'holding'

One point must be emphasised at this stage. The tenant can only ask the court to grant a new lease of the 'holding' he is actually occupying for business purposes. The whole purpose of the Act is to protect tenants who are trading from the property. If the tenant has sublet, it is his subtenants who will each have separate rights under the Act in respect of their separate holdings. If the leaseholder has a tenancy of less than fourteen months to run he ceases to be the 'competent landlord' so far as the subtenants are concerned. They must look to the superior landlord when they wish to claim new leases. That is why it is important for landlords to serve formal notice under section 40 of the 1954 Act requesting full details of all relevant subtenancies before or at the same time as they serve the termination notice.

Who is the occupier?

The time for determining whether the tenant is the occupier of a 'holding' is the date of the court's order. He can lose his rights if he was in occupation during the earlier stages of the renewal process (the notices, the application to the court), but if he has moved out before the moment at which the court actually orders a new tenancy he can lose the Act's protection* (*I. & H. Caplan Ltd* v. *Caplan* (1962)).

The landlord may nevertheless feel that he does not want a multiplicity of subtenants and that it is more convenient to have a single tenant of the entire property. In those circumstances he can, in response to the tenant's court application, call for a tenant who used to have a lease of the whole building but, having sublet the

---

* although his rights can survive so long as 'a thread of continuity' of business use remains unbroken.

rest, is now only occupying part still to take a lease of the entire premises comprised in the old tenancy. In short, the tenant may only demand a new lease of the premises he actually occupies but the landlord may, in effect, elect to grant the tenant a lease comprising either the whole of his original demise or just the portion of the land or building he actually occupies.

There is a special case in which the court may order a new lease of less than the area the tenant previously occupied. This is where the landlord has claimed possession on the ground that he wants to reconstruct but the tenant has indicated his willingness to accept renewal of 'an economically separable part' of his holding and that he is prepared to permit the landlord such facilities as he requires to complete his redevelopment proposals.

The tenant's application to the court

The tenant will generally make an application for the maximum term permitted by the Act unless he has a special reason to opt for a shorter term. The maximum term is fourteen years and the court is not at liberty to order a longer tenancy. The tenant will normally ask for the best terms available so, while he may propose a modest increase to a figure which represents a low estimate of the new market rent, it is common practice simply to ask for the rent that he was paying previously to be repeated on the order of the court. I have not recently come across a tenant applying to pay a lower rent than he was already due to pay, but in some market conditions even this may be reasonable. Unless such exceptional circumstances apply, the figure quoted on the application does not really form part of the negotiations; these go on behind the scenes between the parties or their surveyors. The application is simply to preserve the tenant's rights so that, for instance, a tenant whose twenty-one year lease is just expiring may ask for a new fourteen year term at the same rent with a seven-yearly rent review. Such terms are unlikely to be acceptable to the landlord in modern market conditions.

The application will also normally suggest that the provisions in the new lease should be as in the old lease except for the level of the new rent and the length of the term. Again, there may be some special circumstances (such as the need to carry on a wider use) which may provoke the tenant into asking for this in his application, but it is unusual.

Landlord's need to file an answer

The rules of the County Court say that the landlord must file a formal answer within eight days of the tenant's application. Sometimes, as a preliminary point, the landlord will challenge the validity of the tenant's application. For instance, if the tenant has made an application too late or failed to serve a counter-notice the landlord will say so in the answer and ask for the tenant's application to be struck out. However, it is conveniently the case in English civil proceedings that the landlord is allowed two bites of the cherry by stating that if he is wrong on the procedural point then, in the alternative, he has views on the tenant's application itself. He may, for example have already indicated in his notice that it is his intention to oppose the application and this opposition will be repeated together with the grounds specified in the Act.

In many cases, however, the landlord does not oppose the grant of a new tenancy in principle but, not surprisingly, he does not agree with the terms that the tenant has specified in his application. Typically, in a case where a tenant had asked for a new twenty-one year lease at his old rent of £2000 per annum with seven-yearly reviews, the landlord might say in his answer:

(a) he does not oppose the new tenancy, but
(b) he opposes the following terms proposed by the tenant, namely:
    (i) the term of twenty-one years,
    (ii) rent of £2000 per annum,
    (iii) review every seven years.

In addition, it is quite likely that at the end of a twenty-one year lease the landlord will want to call for the lease to be brought up to date and to incorporate 'modern terms'. In his answer he should therefore specify the particular features of the old lease to which he objects. For instance, if the insurance clause in the old lease was unsatisfactory he would add to the list of items proposed by the tenants to which he takes exception:

    (iv) terms as to insurance to be similar as before.

This would signify his objection to an arrangement by which, in the old lease, the obligation to insure was left with the tenant rather than the modern arrangement by which the landlord insures and recovers the premium (and of course his agency commission on that premium). The fairly limited degree to which the court will agree to vary the terms of the existing lease (other than those relating to rent and the length of the term) was demonstrated by the case of *O'May v. City of London Real Property Co.* (1982) noted in Chapter 1. It is now common practice for the landlord to include in his answer an application for an interim report to be fixed (see below).

Sometimes the landlord fails to file his answer until well after the time limit prescribed. Although theoretically this leaves him in default, it is seldom fatal.

The next stage

The next procedural stage in the County Court is the pre-trial review where the registrar will make orders and directions about the conduct of the proceedings. If the landlord has not filed an answer by then he will be ordered to do so. In addition, the parties will be told how many experts' reports will be required to support their case and, as in any other County Court action, various procedural orders will be made relating to lists of documents and to the trial itself. The equivalent procedure in the High Court takes place at the summons for directions.

In most cases the surveyors representing the parties have taken a back seat during these initial procedural steps, but now the stage is set for the trial of the action they must step forward and occupy a central role in the proceedings. Their most important function is to provide the necessary evidence to assist the court in fixing the new rent. In our adversarial legal system, experts are not called in by the court but by the parties. Each of the parties will enlist the services of one or more persons, usually chartered surveyors practising in the area, who will assemble lists of 'comparables', i.e. lettings involving properties as similar as possible to those comprised in the lease being renewed. It is vital that the details of these comparables are available and that the surveyor is able to prove them so that they may be admissible as evidence at the hearing.

It is essentially the rental value of the property on the open market that is being assessed, not the ability of the property to make money for the tenant's particular business. The tenant's trading figures will therefore normally be disregarded. In *W.J. Barton Ltd* v. *Longacre Securities* (1982) the Court of Appeal was not prepared to accept evidence of the tenant's turnover at a different branch of a baker's shop in North London. The Court will, however, be prepared to look at trading figures at propertics of a special character, such as an hotel or a petrol filling station, where such figures are part of the calculation process by which valuers arrive at their valuations.

Interim rent applications

Under the original scheme of the 1954 Act, the tenant could continue paying the rent required under his old lease until the court's order for the grant of a new lease took effect. This naturally gave the tenant considerable incentive for delay.

We have already seen that one of the major reforms of the 1954 legislation was brought in by the 1969 Law of Property Act. This allows the parties to make a joint application to exclude the renewal provisions (sections 24 to 28) of the 1954 Act. The second important change brought about in 1969 was the introduction of the interim rent provisions under section 24A of the 1954 Act, giving the landlord the opportunity to redress the balance. It is, however, an opportunity which the landlord must take positive steps to assert.

Quite simply, at any time before the hearing date the landlord can apply to the court to fix an interim rent. Once that application has been made (assuming the hearing takes place after the expiry of the date of the lease) the court:

(a) determines the terms of any new tenancy, and
(b) goes on to decide what rent should be paid in the interim period and the date when the old tenancy finally expired.

Since rent continues to be payable at the old rate unless the landlord has made his application, he or his advisers must remember to act well before the date when the old lease is due to expire.

There are sophisticated valuation considerations to be taken into account. The court is expected to fix the rent on the assumption that the tenancy will run from year to year, but it is generally accepted that the interim rent will be about 80% of the final market rent determined by the court. As a procedural matter, the landlord's solicitor can and should apply for the interim rent at the same time that he files his answer. Alternatively, he can make a separate application for an interim rent to be fixed.

It is convenient for the landlord to add his request for an interim rent in his answer as this cuts out the need for a separate set of papers. However, in cases before the County Court there is virtue in making a separate application because it will survive even if for some reason the tenant changes his mind and withdraws his application for a new lease. Thus the landlord can secure an increase in rent for the relevant period even if a new lease is not ultimately granted. Otherwise the proposal for an interim rent could fail when the tenant withdraws his request for a new lease. The landlord's solicitors must remember not merely to issue the application but also to serve it on the tenants or the solicitors within two months, otherwise it will not be valid.

As we saw earlier in this chapter, the tenant may have to apply to the High Court rather than the County Court for his new tenancy. In those circumstances, if the landlord has applied for an interim rent to be fixed by issuing a summons in the tenant's proceedings, his application will survive independently even if the tenant later discontinues his claim (see *Artoc Bank & Trust Ltd* v. *Prudential Assurance plc* (1984)).

Determining the interim rent

An analysis of the cases on interim rents leads to the conclusion that where the new rent is substantially higher than the old rent the court will 'have regard to' the old rent by adjusting the new rent downwards by 10%. Also, where the new tenancy is not to be a very short lease or subject to an early option to determine it, the courts have accepted the views of valuers that the assumption they are required to make when fixing the interim rent – of a tenancy from year to year – produces a further reduction of 10% as compared with the new rent. Thus the total deduction is indeed 20% in the majority of cases.

The interim rent will continue until three months after the application is finally disposed of, so after allowing six weeks time for appeal to elapse this means that the interim rent period can last from the date when the original lease expires (or the date of the landlord's interim rent application, if this was later) until four and a half months after the court hearing. Clearly, where large sums are involved (as with a new rent of £100,000 and an interim rent of £80,000) the tenant has a considerable financial inducement to prolong the process of court hearings and appeals. However, the tenant abusing the process in this way could be caught out if there is a rising market as the rent ultimately settled by the court could be higher at the end of a protracted period. Where substantial sums are not involved, the tenant will usually be reluctant to go to the expense of a hearing. The landlord should respond to the tenant's delaying tactics in such circumstances by stating that he will only concede an interim rent if the case goes to court.

The discount represented by the interim rent means that it is always the landlord who must force the pace of any Landlord and Tenant Act negotiation. He should not allow the tenant to prevaricate. Of course, where no interim rent application has been made the tenant has no real incentive to agree a new lease as the new rental will normally be substantially more than the old. A solicitor who has failed to advise a landlord to make an interim rent application would almost certainly be found to be negligent.

The hearing

The majority of cases never reach court. They are settled or abandoned before the point where a judge actually hears the parties and their evidence. But many cases do get heard and a casual glance at the weekly property press or the contents page of the Law Reports will show the very large number of cases where litigation relating to the Landlord and Tenant Act has taken place. At its basic level the court is there to determine the rent according to the expert evidence it receives. The court will also consider requests by the parties for new terms to be incorporated in the tenancy. It may also have to determine whether the tenant is entitled to a new tenancy at all or if one of the grounds asserted by the landlord is valid and allows the application to be successfully opposed.

The new tenancy

Duration

The court has the power to order that the new tenancy shall be for a term that it considers 'reasonable in all the circumstances' but does not exceed fourteen years. This new term will begin at the end of the current tenancy and usually the court will order a term of the same number of years as the old lease. However, although the new *term* will start from the termination date specified in the termination notice (served by the landlord under section 25 or by the tenant under section 26) the new *rent* will only start on the date the old tenancy finally expires under section 64, i.e. three months after the matter is finally disposed of. Until then, only the interim rent will be payable and, if the landlord forgot to ask for it, the rent under the old lease. This has important implications as regards the dates for rent reviews and eventual expiry of the new lease.

Other terms

These are again determined by the court but this time the court has 'regard to the terms of the current tenancy and to all relevant circumstances'. It was this provision in section 35 that was litigated up to the House of Lords in the case of *O'May* v. *City of London Real Property Company* (1982) which we have already considered in Chapter 1 and earlier in this chapter. The effect of that decision was that either party is able to resist any changes in the terms of the lease (except, of course, rent and duration) that impose upon him any greater obligations than the current tenancy. This has led some negotiators in the field to tell their clients: 'If you really want or need the change, then you probably won't get it. If you don't really want or need the change, there is no point in going to court to get it!'

Rent reviews

Section 34(3) was inserted into the 1954 Act by the Law of Property Act 1969. This says:

'The court may, if it thinks fit, further determine that the terms of the tenancy shall include such provision for varying the rent as may be specified in the determination.'

In practice, the court will always include a rent review where the lease is to be of any length and the frequency of reviews will follow market practice as established by evidence. Although there is overwhelming evidence that rent reviews negotiated in the open market are 'upwards only', the courts have adopted the principle that reviews should be in either direction.

As to the assumptions to be included in the review clause for the purpose of fixing the rent there is, surprisingly, no case law at present. However, it seems reasonable to assume that the court would be bound to incorporate the same definition of market value as the 1954 Act already incorporates in section 34 (see below) and that it would be unlikely to order a lease that contained time traps. The courts do not seem yet to have resolved what is to happen to review clauses in current leases that are now coming up for renewal. This could provoke some litigation, although I suspect most parties are content to live with the old clauses and do not choose to raise the point.

Rent

Because section 34 links the rental to the terms of the new tenancy, the terms the new lease is to contain relating to assigning and subletting, permitted use, rent reviews, and any break clause are all factors to be taken into account. The rental must be that at which 'the holding might reasonably be expected to be let in the open market by a willing lessor'. No 'willing tenant' is mentioned, but perhaps this is self-evident by virtue of the tenant's application even though the tenant is not to be regarded as being in occupation.

Matters disregarded in fixing new rent

Matters disregarded are the tenant's occupation of the holding (but not necessarily the occupation of subtenants or the tenant's occupation of an adjacent building); goodwill attaching by reason of the tenant's business or that of his predecessor (but not the goodwill of a subtenant's business nor, necessarily, that attaching to the tenant's adjacent property); and, in the case of licensed premises, the value attaching to the licence.

Improvements only qualify to be disregarded if the tenant or his predecessor (but *not* his subtenant) carried them out otherwise than pursuant to an obligation to his immediate landlord. In addition, the improvement must have been carried out *either* during the current tenancy *or* during the twenty-one years before the tenant applied to the court. During that time the tenancies must always have been business tenancies as defined by the Act and at no time must the term have reverted back to the landlord. It will be remembered that certain improvements qualify for compensation under the 1927 Act. To be disregarded for rental purposes on the renewal under the 1954 Act the same conditions do not apply. In particular, the tenant need not have obtained consent.

The basic rule under section 64 of the 1954 Act is that the existing tenancy will continue until three months 'after the application has been finally disposed of' so that apart from the tenant's obligation to pay an interim rent (if the landlord has applied for it) the terms of the old lease will survive until that point.

Tenant changes his mind

It may happen that after applying to the court for a new tenancy the tenant decides that he does not after all want a new lease. If his application was to the County Court he merely has to file a notice of discontinuance. This brings the action to an end and the tenancy will expire three months later. If the application was in the High Court it is necessary to ask for leave to withdraw the proceedings. The court will consider if the landlord has been prejudiced.

This arose in the case of *Lloyds Bank plc* v. *City of London Corporation* (1983). Lloyds' lease of their branch at 3 Broad Street ran out on 18 December 1980. They put in a tenant's request for a new lease and the landlords served a counter-notice stating that they would oppose this on the grounds of proposed redevelopment. In July 1980 the landlords withdrew their opposition but meanwhile Lloyds had made an internal policy decision not to seek renewal after all. They advised the Corporation of their decision in October 1980, indicating that a six month extension of their tenancy would suffice. In 1981 they applied to the High Court to withdraw their application. The Corporation argued that the court should give leave to withdraw the application on condition that Lloyds would waive their claim for compensation which on the old twice rateable value basis worked out at £65,776. But the court decided that Lloyds could withdraw without forfeiting the compensation in the absence of some other prejudice to the landlord.

It may be that once the terms of the new lease are determined the tenant does not find them favourable even though he applied for renewal in the first place. In that case the tenant has fourteen days in which to apply to the court for the order to be revoked. It is also open to the parties to agree that they will not act on the court's order and to bring the tenancy to an end at a mutually convenient point.

Compensation for disturbance

The tenant will not get compensation if the landlord is seeking possession on the ground that the tenant has been 'a bad tenant', i.e. on grounds (a), (b) or (c) of section 30 of the Act. These are the cases where the tenant has persistently failed to repair or pay rent promptly or has been in breach of other covenants in the lease. Compensation is also not available where the landlord offered satisfactory alternative accommodation (ground (d)).

However, where the tenant has, in effect, been 'a good tenant' and the landlord is seeking possession for his own purposes under ground(e), the landlord wants to lease the whole and not renew a sublease, (f) the landlord intends to demolish or reconstruct, (g) the landlord requires the property for his own occupation, then the tenant is entitled to claim compensation. This right can be excluded where the tenant or a business he has taken over has not been there for five years, but otherwise it cannot be excluded by agreement.

Originally compensation was based on the tenant receiving the rateable value of his holding if he had been in occupation for a period not exceeding fourteen years, or twice the rateable value if his occupation exceeded fourteen years. This has now been modified by the Landlord and Tenant Act (Appropriate Multiplier) Regulations 1981 and is at present three times or six times the rateable value respectively. In working out the period of occupation the tenant can use occupation by his predecessors in the same business. In practical terms, this means that if he bought the good-will of the previous owner's business he can aggregate the period with his own.

Normally the compensation will be in respect of the portion of the building occupied by him although an interesting decision was made in the case of *Edicron* v. *William Whiteley Limited* (1984) where the Court of Appeal held that although the tenant had sublet at various points during the fourteen year period he could still claim compensation in respect of the entire holding.

Compensation for improvements

We have already seen that the tenant can get compensation for having to leave his premises if the landlord has established a right to recover possession on certain specified grounds. This is compensation for disturbance. There is, however, a separate head of compensation for improvements, and this derives not from the 1954 Act but from the earlier Landlord and Tenant Act 1927. This Act not only allows tenants to carry out certain classes of improvement even if the lease prohibits them, but also allows him to claim compensation at the end of the term. However, to get that compensation he must have followed a strict procedure at the time those improvements were carried out.

To qualify, the improvements proposed by a business tenant must have been carried out more than three years before the termination of the tenancy, they must be of a kind that would add to the letting value of the premises, and they must be reasonable and suitable to the character of the building. Moreover, they should not have an adverse effect on the value of adjoining property belonging to the same landlord.

To claim the benefit of the Act the tenant must serve the landlord with notice of his intention to carry out the improvements together with a suitable specification and plan. The landlord has three months to object to the proposal or, alternatively, to offer to carry out the improvements himself in return for a reasonable increase of rent. If he does not so offer but persists in objecting to the tenant's proposal, the tenant has the right to ask the court for a certificate that his proposed improvement is a proper one.

It must often happen that the tenant does not have the compensation provisions of the 1927 Act in mind when requesting consent for alterations. However, even if he or his advisers failed to give notice of the proposals in a formal way, making express reference to the Act in his notice, the improvements may still qualify for compensation claims. This occurred in the case of *Deerfield Travel Services Ltd* v. *Leathersellers Co.* (1982). There the High Court judge ordered that the tenant's notice was a good one if a reasonable recipient would have regarded it as notice of intention to carry out the work. The Court of Appeal agreed and made it clear that the notice could qualify even if the plan and specifications required by the 1927 Act were served on the landlord at different times or, provided the plan contained sufficient detail, if there were no specifications at all.

It follows that if after the tenant has served his notice requesting the right to carry out the improvements the landlord does not object (or offer to do the improvements himself) or, alternatively, if the court grants the tenant the certificate for which he has asked, then the tenant can go ahead and carry out his improvements.

What the tenant can claim

At the end of the tenancy and when the tenant leaves he will then be entitled to claim *either* the net addition to the holding or the *cost* of carrying out the improvements at the end of the term *less* the cost of putting the premises into repair. It must, however, be borne in mind that if the landlord has established an intention to demolish or reconstruct the premises the improvements may be of nil value for compensation purposes.

When to claim

Where the tenant has gone through the necessary procedure at the time the improvements were made, there are further strict requirements to be met before he can make a valid claim for this kind of compensation. If the landlord terminated the current business tenancy by service of a section 25 notice, the tenant must apply for compensation within three months from the date that notice was given. However, where termination has arisen as a result of a tenant's request for a new tenancy the three months run from the date of the landlord's counter-notice. If the landlord did not serve a counter-notice then the time limit for claiming compensation is two months from the date that the tenant made his request.

If the tenancy merely expires by effluxion of time (as might happen where the tenancy is too short for the 1954 Act to apply or where it had been deliberately excluded), then the tenant must make his claim for compensation between three and six months before the tenancy ends.

Where the tenancy is forfeited or the landlord re-enters, the claim must be made within three months of the effective date of the court order or, if there is no court order, three months from the date of re-entry.

In making his claim the tenant must set out his full name and address (and that of the landlord), a description of the holding and his business, details of his claim for compensation and of the improvements (including the date they were completed and their costs), and a statement of the amount he claims is due.

Where a landlord exercises the option to carry out the improvements requested by the tenant and then carries out the work, he is entitled to a reasonable increase in rent. There appear to be no cases interpreting 'reasonable' in this context. Is it the improved market value that is payable or is it an increase based on cost plus a reasonable rate of return?

The tenant may decide to involve the court at the time the improvements are requested, when he would ask for a certificate that they are proper improvements. Alternatively, the tenant may do so if, at the time of his claim for compensation, the landlord objects. The application will be a claim either to the High Court or the County Court according to the rateable value of the holding.

Problems arise when a subtenant has carried out the improvement. The subtenant has a claim for compensation against his own landlord but the intermediate landlord does not have a corresponding claim against the superior landlord. Accordingly, where a subtenant applies for consent to carry out improvements the intermediate landlord should elect to carry out the works in order to preserve his right to get compensation from his own landlord at the end of the term. Perhaps he could appoint the subtenant to act as his project manager!

What the tenant must leave behind

When the tenant finally leaves the premises at which he has carried on a business for a number of years, what can he take with him and what must he leave behind? He is not at liberty to strip the premises and leave a shell. Basically fixtures, including those he has installed himself, become part of the landlord's building and must be left behind. This would, of course, be a most unreasonable rule if there were no exceptions.

It is well established that tenants' fixtures and articles resting on the land by their own weight and not fixed to it do not form part of the land and may be removed. The tenant may do this within a reasonable time after the end of a periodic tenancy (e.g. weekly or monthly) but he must remove them before the end of a fixed term. If articles were already fixed to the premises before the lease commenced, they will be treated as landlord's fixtures, even if they were installed by a former tenant who failed to remove them.

Quite large objects have been judged to be removable fixtures: a wooden barn (*R.* v. *Londonthorpe Inhabitants* (1795)), or a windmill (*R.* v. *Otley Inhabitants Suffolk* (1830)) were tenants' fixtures because they were standing by their own weight, even though the foundations beneath them were let into the ground. Other old cases held that tramlines fastened to sleepers which were merely laid on the ground were not fixtures (*Duke of Beaufort* v. *Bates* (1862)) but railway sand or ballast were fixtures (*Turner* v. *Cameron* (1890)).

However, if it can be shown that the article or chattel was fixed to the structure of the premises to enable the object itself to be used more effectively then the act of fixing does not compel the tenant to leave it behind as a landlord's fixture. Thus the tenant was allowed to remove petrol pumps in the case of *Smith* v. *City Petroleum Co. Ltd* (1940).

Staying on

Of course a tenant will often stay in possession after his lease expires. He may simply be 'holding over' or he may be in the process of renewing his tenancy by negotiation or under the Landlord and Tenant Act 1954. In these circumstances it would be unfair for him to lose his fixtures because he failed to remove them before the formal expiry of his old lease.

The courts have now made it clear that not only does the tenant have the right to remove fixtures in the holding over period but also after a new lease is granted, even if the grant is treated as forming a surrender of the old lease by operation of law. This rule was affirmed by the Court of Appeal in *New Zealand Government Property Corporation* v. *H M & S Ltd* (1982). The lease of Her Majesty's Theatre in London had run out in 1970 but in 1973 a new lease was granted for twenty-one years from 1970 with seven-yearly reviews. It was at the first review that the point of law was raised as to whether, for instance, the seats in the theatre had become the landlord's rather than the tenant's fixtures as a result of the failure to remove them when the old lease was surrendered in 1973. Lord Denning considered that the rent should be assessed on the basis that the tenant could have removed the seats and other fixtures had he wished to do so, and that they had remained the tenant's property.

It should be stressed that the parties are at liberty to specify in the lease (or some collateral agreement) what particular articles are to be treated as landlord's or tenant's fixtures, and where a tenant is proposing to extend it is a sound idea to clear the air and establish the position at the outset.

Chapter 12

Licensees, service occupiers and other hybrids

Why not grant a tenancy?

Why should landlords sometimes wish to grant a licence rather than a lease or a tenancy agreement? The motive may be a wish to avoid various statutory provisions which apply to tenancies but not to licences (what one might call statutory reasons) or it may be dictated by the facts of the specific situation (practical reasons).

In the field of residential occupation the statutory reasons are extremely persuasive. A valid licence is not caught by the provisions of the Rent Acts either as regards security of tenure or limitation of rents. In *Somma* v. *Hazelhurst* (1978), the court held that separate non-exclusive licence agreements granted to the residential occupier of a room were definitely outside the Rent Acts, and in the Court of Appeal Lord Justice Cumming-Bruce assisted all landlords of residential accommodation even further by spelling out the wording of the licence which proved so effective in the body of his judgment. See also *Street* v. *Mountford* (1984).

In commercial premises, landlords often wish to create tenancies which are outside the workings of the 1954 Landlord and Tenant Act in order to guarantee recovery of possession at the end of the lease. Since 1969 the need to dress up such a tenancy as a licence is much reduced because the parties may simply contract out of the renewal provisions of the 1954 Act (sections 24 to 28) under the procedure outlined in Chapter 11.

The contracting out procedure can be a bit of a nuisance, so when landlords are proposing to grant a tenancy for a few months they sometimes tell their legal advisers to 'draw up a short form of licence to cover the situation'. This can cause pitfalls since it is not what the document is called that matters but the nature of the transaction as a whole – although the intentions of the parties are also relevant.

Contrasting leases and licences

The essential difference between a lease and a licence is that a lease
or tenancy grants the tenant 'a proprietary interest' in the land, not
just a personal right of occupation. The right to exclusive possession
of land was at one time thought to be the distinctive feature of a
tenancy, but various cases have demonstrated that this is not
necessarily so. In *Street* v. *Mountford* (1984) the Court of Appeal
accepted that Mrs Mountford had been given the exclusive
occupation of rooms in a house in Boscombe. But the licence
contained provisions which the court considered unusual in a
tenancy agreement, such as a prohibition on children or keeping
pets. However, the position is by no means clear from the landlord's
point of view.

Even where the parties strenuously avoid 'tenancy-like' words and
call themselves 'the grantor' and 'grantee', the court may still decide
whether or not it is a licence. This happened in a case involving the
letting of a tennis court club house (see *Addiscombe Garden Estates
Ltd* v. *Crabbe* (1957)). Accordingly, where there is any doubt at all
the landlord who wants to be sure of regaining possession of
commercial premises would do better to apply to contract out of the
1954 Act than to take a chance and call the document 'a licence'.

Short tenancies

Very short tenancies of business premises fall outside the 1954 Act.
Thus a tenancy for a term not exceeding six months is not within the
statute provided that the tenant (or his predecessor in business) has
not been in occupation for a period exceeding twelve months in all.
Moreover, the agreement must not contain provisions for its own
renewal beyond a six month period.

It follows that a short tenancy for up to six months can safely be
granted and it can then be renewed once. But if the tenant has
remained in occupation for more than twelve months he will qualify
for the Act's protection. So if, as the twelve month period draws to a
close, the tenant seems likely to stay it will be necessary to formalise
the position by an application to the court. Otherwise, if the tenancy
extends beyond the end of the second six month period and the
landlord accepts rent beyond that period the whole tenancy will
come beneath the umbrella of the 1954 Act. As an alternative the

landlord can require the tenant to give up possession for one day at the end of twelve months and then grant a new short lease.

Licence of shared accommodation

There may, however, be practical reasons why a licence is both necessary and justifiable. The particular instance that comes most readily to mind is where the landlord retains the right to the use of part of the premises so that there is a genuine sharing of accommodation. A typical example might be the licensing of a kiosk within a larger store. The landlord has at no time given up possession of his store or any part of it, but has permitted an outsider to carry on business in a designated portion of the premises. It is almost always characteristic of such a licence that it will be personal to the licensee and, unlike most leases, will not be assignable.

Service occupiers

In dealing with service occupancies we are straying once more into the field of the residential tenancy. Whether someone living in part of a commercial property is a genuine service occupier can be an important consideration for the landlord and his mortgagee. It may often happen that an employee or manager is required to live 'over the shop' and a landlord who is keen to preserve the commercial nature of his property investment will be anxious to know that in permitting such an occupation he is not opening the flood gates to the Rent Acts and all that they entail.

These Acts do not apply so long as the employee is occuping the property strictly as a mere licensee. To qualify, the employee must be *required* as a term of his contract of employment to occupy the specified premises 'for the better performance of his duties'. The service contract will therefore state that the tenant's right of occupation will come to an end when his employment comes to an end. The safer course seems to be that there should be no rent chargeable, although there is no objection to the employee's remuneration being adjusted by reference to the fact that he has been provided with accommodation.

It follows that the landlord should not be too worried about permitting his business tenants to allow employees rights of occupation in this way. Leases which permit this would normally contain such words as:

'Not to use the premises for residential purposes except upon a bona fide service occupancy to which the provisions of the Rent Acts conferring security of tenure shall not apply.'

If the occupier turns out after all to be a tenant the position is different, although from the landlord's viewpoint all is not quite lost. He will have to persuade the court that the residential accommodation 'is reasonably required . . . for occupation as a residence for some person engaged in his whole time employment' and that the contract of employment of the outgoing tenant, to whom the flat had been let in consequence of that employment, has been terminated (Case 8 to Schedule 15 of the Rent Act 1977). But recovery of possession is discretionary as this is one of the grounds where the court *may* order possession but is not obliged to do so.

The subtenant will be protected

Of course, a Rent Act protected tenancy will certainly arise where a business tenant sublets a portion of the building to a residential sub-tenant. Thus the holder of the headlease will continue to be bound by the Landlord and Tenant Act 1954 but the subtenant will enjoy the same right to be protected from eviction and to have a fair rent fixed as any other regulated tenant and the regulated tenancy will be binding on the landlord when the headlease ends.

Other mixed uses

There are two further cases in which there is a residential element in what is essentially a commercial building. The most obvious is where the entire premises are let to one tenant who lives personally 'over the shop' and whose lease allows him to do so.

At one time there was considerable doubt as to whether the tenant occupying mixed premises of this kind as his home might not be able to avail himself of the considerable protection afforded by the Rent Act. In one way, the law is clear. Section 24(3) of the Rent Act 1977 says:

'A tenancy shall be not a regulated tenancy (i.e. protected by the Act) if it is a tenancy to which Part II of the Landlord and Tenant Act 1954 applies.'

As the 1954 Act covers premises 'all or part of which are used for a business carried on by the tenant', it seems that the 1954 Act will apply so long as there is a definite business use of some part of the property. As you might expect, however, there are some grey areas. A doctor who carried on practice from home but who also had consulting rooms elsewhere has been held not to be carrying on a business use and was consequently protected by the Rent Acts (*Royal Life Saving Society* v. *Page* (1979)). But an importer of sea food, working from home with no other premises, was held to be carrying on a business (*Cheryl Investments Limited* v. *Saldanha* (1979)).

According to the Court of Appeal the test is whether, as in the case of the doctor, his work was merely incidental to the residential occupation or, as in the case of the importer, it was a significant purpose of the occupation. But a business use in breach of the terms of the tenancy will not get the 1954 Act protection unless the landlord has approved or acquiesced in it.

A different position arises if the tenant has ceased to carry on business at the premises and merely goes on living in the residential portion. This might happen, for instance, because a tenant formerly carrying on a business has fallen ill and is forced to retire but continues to live in the upper part of the premises. The pressure of modern rentals is such that he could probably not afford to do this for long, so perhaps the situation will not arise too often. Another possibility, however, is that the landlord might have allowed a subletting of the business portion of the premises leaving the main tenant in residence in the upper parts. In such cases there is a strong likelihood that the tenant would acquire rights under the Rent Acts, and landlords should accordingly be on their guard.

Can the landlord refuse consent?

If the lease requires landlord's consent to a subletting but contains no prohibition on residential use, is the landlord being unreasonable if he refuses consent on the sole ground that the subletting would be protected by the Rent Acts? In *West Layton* v. *Ford* (1979) the lease had been granted in 1971 and permitted furnished sublettings which, at that time, were not protected by the Rent Acts. Lord Denning considered that the statutory background (i.e. the change in the law in 1974 which protected furnished tenants) was a matter against which the question of reasonableness should be considered. In the circumstances of that case, the landlord was justified in refusing his consent to sublet at a time after the Rent Act 1974 was enacted. The position could well be different where the law has not changed since the outset of the tenancy. In some cases the landlord has succeeded and in others he has not. Each case will be considered on its particular facts.

Leasehold Reform Act

The rights of long leaseholders of residential property intruded into the commercial section in a case heard by the House of Lords in 1982, *Tandon* v. *Spurgeon's Homes*. There, the tenant held under a long lease at a low rent as defined by the Leasehold Reform Act 1967. The premises were primarily business premises (by area) although the tenant did live in a two storey maisonette. What the court had to decide was whether the building comprised in this lease was a 'house, properly so called' because the 1967 Act applies only to dwelling houses and not to flats. The court held that for the purposes of the Act the building was a 'house' and the long leaseholder could insist on acquiring the freehold. Moreover, the fact that the tenant also qualified as a business tenant for the purposes of the 1954 Act was irrelevant.

This appeared to be a fairly unusual set of circumstances but it must occur frequently enough because a considerable flurry was caused when the case was finally decided.

Whilst it is unusual to find a long leaseholder in occupation of an entire building and using part for business purposes, rights equivalent to those considered in the Spurgeon's Homes case could arise even where the business portion has been sublet by the leaseholder. Suppose a building consisting of a shop and upper parts is held on a ninety-nine year lease and some time ago the tenant or his predecessor sublet the shop portion for commercial use but continued to reside in the remainder. For the purposes of the 1967 Leasehold Reform Act, he is still 'in possession' of the business portion because he is in receipt of the rents. He is still the leaseholder of the entire building, and because he lives in the flat the building is a 'house properly so called'. Even in those circumstances, which do not seem to be what Parliament envisaged, he would have a right to claim enfranchisement and either extend his lease or buy the freehold.

To qualify under the Leasehold Reform Act the property must have a rateable value within the prescribed limits, at present £1500 in London and £750 elsewhere.

Chapter 13

The Land Registry: is registration required?

The Land Registry maintains a state guaranteed register of titles affecting land in many parts of the country. Business leases often do not require registration at the Land Registry because they are too short. However, the consequences of failing to register a lease which does qualify for registration are serious so the provisions of the Land Registration Acts (1925–1971) as they apply to leases must be borne in mind.

Land registration is compulsory in London and most large towns and cities in England and Wales, and compulsory registration is gradually being extended to all parts of the country. In addition, there are pieces of land which are not in compulsory areas but which owners were able to register by 'voluntary application', a procedure that has for the time being been suspended except for special cases. Thus the need to register a lease can arise outside the compulsory areas.

The essential rules

The essential rules for leases are:

(a) A lease for a term not exceeding twenty-one years does not need to be registered at all because it is an 'overriding interest'.
(b) A new lease granted for a term of not less than forty years must be registered if the land is in a compulsory area.
(c) If an existing lease has not less than forty years to run at the date it is assigned then it must be registered if it is in a compulsory registration area.
(d) If the landlord's title is already registered then the tenant must apply to register any lease for a term exceeding twenty-one years whether or not it is in a compulsory area.

The tenant's application to register must be made within two months or it is void. The position is not irretrievable and late applications can be made but it is possible for third parties to acquire rights against the land in the intervening period.

I have already mentioned certain circumstances in which such interests as options or pre-emption clauses require registration. Where the land against which the interest is to be registered has a Land Registry title, the interest or contract must be entered as a notice or caution at the appropriate District Land Registry. Where the land is unregistered, registration of these interests against the name of the proprietor (not against the land) is carried out by the Land Charges Registry in Plymouth.

Land Registry fees on leases are generally moderate, but they are one factor which should be considered in deciding whether to grant or accept a new lease for a term exceeding twenty-one years.

Chapter 14

Rates and taxes

Rates

A tenancy is said to be 'inclusive' of rates where the landlord has agreed to pay them and 'exclusive' where they are the tenant's liability. Most commercial leases are drafted so as to place liability on the tenant's shoulders, and where the premises have a separate rating assessment this is not normally a problem. With a few exceptions, any agreement the parties reach on the subject will be enforceable by the courts. The relevant clause will generally be to 'pay all rates taxes and other outgoings whether or not of an annual or recurring nature'. This clearly includes liability to general and water rates, and such items as charges for making up a private road under the Highways Act 1980 would also be caught by a broadly worded covenant. Liabilities which, in the context of the lease, are connected with the landlord's repairing obligations are likely to remain with the landlord.

Rates are normally the responsibility of the occupier but section 58 of the General Rate Act 1957 does allow the local authority to levy them on the owner where the property has only a small rateable value. A tenant of premises for a term not exceeding three months is entitled by statute (section 58 of the General Rate Act) to deduct rates from the rent paid to the owner. In practice, when there is a very short term tenancy it will be drafted so as to be 'inclusive of rates', with the landlord adjusting the rent to take account of this. Otherwise as rates are not a charge on the property, a landlord is not bound to pay the rates of a defaulting tenant.

Where the lease is on inclusive terms and the rates rise after the tenant has carried out improvements as defined by the Landlord and Tenant Act 1927 (see Chapter 10), the tenant must refund the increase. (This applies to an increased fire insurance premium too. See section 16 of the Landlord and Tenant Act 1927.)

Income tax

Like any other income, the income of property, i.e. rent, is subject to the imposition of income tax at whatever rates are applicable to the taxpayer. Income from land is tax under Schedule A of the Income and Corporation Taxes Act 1970. (A company's income is liable for corporation tax.)

It is, of course, 'the annual profits or gains arising' in respect of rent and receipts on which the tax is levied, and not the gross rent. The principal expenses the landlord can deduct from the gross rental he receives are:

(a) Cost of maintenance repairs and insurance. The insurance must relate to the property not, for instance, a sinking fund policy. There is a view that insuring loss of rent may not be allowable.
(b) Services he is obliged to provide but for which he is not paid separately. 'Obliged' does not necessarily mean obliged by the lease. It can just mean obliged by commonsense or good estate management.
(c) Rates or other payments charged on the land.
(d) Ground rent payable to the superior landlord.

Expenditure on the common parts of the building are allowable expenses under these headings.

If the tenant makes a payment intended to cover repair and maintenance costs for work which the lease does not oblige him to carry out, it may be treated as rent in the hands of the landlord. If the tenant defaults in paying his rent, the landlord must claim relief against tax on the sum he did not receive and must show that he took reasonable steps to enforce payment or (if he waived payment voluntarily) that it was reasonable to avoid hardship and without 'consideration', e.g. a payment of some kind from the tenant.

If a lease of fifty years or less is granted at a premium this will, in part, be treated as rent and taxed as such. It is worked out by reducing the amount of the premium by one fiftieth for each year (less one year) of the lease. So if a twenty-one year lease is granted at a premium of £10,000, the landlord will be charged income tax on £10,000, less £200 × 20, i.e. £10,000 − £4000 = £6000. If hardship can be proved, the tax may be paid by instalments over not more than eight years.

Capital gains tax

Payment of a premium can also be treated as a part disposal of an asset under the Capital Gains Taxes Act 1979. Otherwise, the grant of a lease is not in itself a disposal for capital gains tax purposes. The disposal of an existing lease for a term of less than fifty years (and this can include a licence) is deemed to be a disposal of a 'wasting asset', under which special rules apply, in order to restrict the allowances which it is permissible to set against the sale price for the purpose of computing the gain and hence the tax due.

Capital transfer tax

This is in essence a tax on gifts and will not, therefore, be affected by routine grants or assignments of commercial leases 'at arm's length'. It should, however, be mentioned in passing that where, say, a family business is handed down from one generation to the next, a commercial lease may be part of business property and there could be some relief available from the tax. (See section 73 of the Finance Act 1976.)

Development land tax

This tax is levied on the development element on the disposal of land. The grant or assignment of a lease is treated as a part disposal. Liability arises where there is 'realised development value'.

Put at its simplest (a dangerous practice in the tax field), tax at the current rate of 60% will be payable on the amount by which the *consideration* for the property exceeds 115% of its *current use value* or, alternatively, 115% of its *acquisition cost*. Both these concepts have been defined at length by the 1976 Finance Act which has, in turn, been extensively amended by subsequent Finance Acts. There is an exemption for the first £75,000 of realised development value.

On the sale or grant of a lease, the value of the 'right to rents' is added to the premium in order to calculate the consideration element. A charge to tax is most likely to occur when a substantial premium or increased rent is obtained following the grant or prospect of planning permission which enhances the value of the land. Where the disposal is the grant of a lease, the landlord may elect to pay the tax in ten annual instalments and is not required to pay interest on the unpaid balance.

All this brief outline can do is draw the reader's attention to the existence of the tax. If there seems to be any possibility of the tax arising, it is vital to obtain specialist advice.

Value added tax

This is a tax on the supply of goods and services. By Schedule 5 of the Finance Act 1972, in almost all circumstances payment of rent will not attract VAT. By that section the grant, assignment or surrender of any interest or agreement over land is exempt. Possibly the supply of services by a landlord, if on a scale to rise above the current VAT exemption limit (£18,300 in 1984/5), could be taxable. For instance, cleaning services supplied by a landlord would be taxable but the supply of heating is zero rated. A businessman selling the goodwill of his business would not have to charge VAT on the sale price of the lease but would have to impose VAT on the fixtures, fittings and stock in trade, although there are self cancelling arrangements under the VAT regulations where the purchaser is also registered for VAT. Finally, VAT will be payable on services of the landlord's advisers, his solicitors, estate agents, valuers and so forth, and this is so even though the client is not resident in this country if the land in question is located in the UK.

VAT is not levied upon service charges, but a service charge will almost certainly include some elements upon which VAT has been paid. If the landlord is a 'trader' able to offset all of his VAT payments against his receipts, the service charge should be calculated net of the VAT included on any item. More usually, the landlord's major source of income will be rents, dividends and interest and he will be unable to set off VAT payments. In such a case he will have to include the VAT he has paid in calculating the total service charge due from his tenants. This can be unfair to the tenant who is registered for VAT because he will be unable to offset against his own VAT liability the VAT hidden within the global service charge calculation.

Now that most building works are subject to VAT this has become a significant problem. It would seem that the only way tenants can overcome the unnecessary burden is to offer to carry out the works themselves.

Stamp duty

Stamp duty is one of our oldest taxes. There is a scale of rates
applicable to leases which rises according to the amount of the rent
and the term. The rate of duty is greater if the lease is for a term
exceeding seven years and is greater again if it exceeds thirty-five
and 100 years respectively. A tenant taking a commercial lease for a
little more than seven or a little more than thirty-five years should
bear this in mind. Stamp duty is charged on the average rent, but if
the amount cannot be ascertained (as in the case of a review to
market rent) the lease is treated for stamp duty purposes as being at
the original rent throughout the whole of the term.

Where a premium is charged, it is liable for stamp duty in just the
same way as a conveyance. If the lease contains a certificate of value
(declaring that it does not form part of a series of transactions, etc.)
then no duty is payable until the premium rises above £30,000.
Thereafter it would be at the rate of 1% under the 1984 Finance Act
(which also removed a number of ingenious schemes that sought to
make stamp duty an 'optional tax').

Where there is an agreement to grant a lease for a term not
exceeding thirty-five years, the agreement itself is stamped as if it
were a lease. If the lease is subsequently granted a fixed duty of five
pence is payable, but if the agreement falls through there is no
refund available. The counterpart lease (the part signed by the
tenant but not by the landlord) bears stamp duty of fifty pence only.

Under the Stamp Act 1891 it is actually a criminal offence not to
pay stamp duty on a lease, but the principal motive for stamping any
legal document is that if it is not properly stamped it is not
admissible as evidence in court. In order to discourage people from
stamping documents only when litigation is pending the Stamp Duty
Office will impose a penalty if it suspects that this is the reason for
failing to pay stamp duty promptly.

Chapter 15

Recent trends and the future

Those involved in creating business tenancies ignore at their peril the wider world of business itself. Commercial leases are by no means a sensitive indicator of the temperature of the economy as a whole. Nor do they reflect social or economic trends. But they do react to them and, even if legislation does not intervene, subtle changes in the business tenancy market take place to reflect the wider social and economic scene.

The changing pattern

Let us imagine the developer of a parade of suburban shops – a piece of typical ribbon development along the trunk roads of the 1930s. It would have been natural for him to grant a twenty-one year lease of each shop at a fixed rental of, say, £300 per annum. He would have had no conception of the turmoil which the world as a whole, including the property and business world, was to undergo as a result first of World War II itself and its austere aftermath, and then of the gradual recovery blossoming into the boom of the 1950s. All this would have taken place during the term of the first of the leases granted in that parade.

Take our developer or perhaps his son renewing those leases in the mid 1950s. Again, he grants a fourteen year term on a fixed rent of around £850. In ten years his investment will have a distinctly 'reversionary' look; by 1965 market rents would be running at about £1500 per annum for the same parade of shops.

Our original developer's son or grandson renews those leases once more in the late 1960s. This time he is wiser and provides for a rent review after seven or even five years. At least he has a chance on each review of rescuing his investment from the ravages of inflation. But the lease was granted at a time of near full employment, whilst at the end our mythical landlord is lucky if his tenants have remained solvent, particularly if his premises are in one of the depressed areas with nearly half the working population unemployed. Early in the 70s he had to endure the 'business rent freeze' imposed by the Heath government as part of its prices and incomes policy. Paradoxically, it is a Labour government which implements decontrol. Will our builder's grandson or great grandson renewing the leases once more be perceptive enough to protect his interests and that of his family effectively for another fourteen or twenty-one years?

The recession

One result of the recession has been widely recognised. This is the desire on the part of tenants to take shorter leases and often to do so in smaller units. The collapse of large companies and the shedding of workers with fairly substantial redundancy payments, which they put into starting new businesses, has added to the number of entrepreneurs looking for small business premises. The influx of immigrants from the Commonwealth, particularly those of Asian origin, skilled in small business and willing to work hard at it has also inflated the demand for the small business unit, either workshop or corner shop, whilst it is the large warehouses and factory units that can be in danger of lying empty.

Upwards only rent reviews

The universal adoption of the 'upwards only' rent review has meant that the virture of a long lease, which in the old days gave a businessman certainty and continuity, is now out-weighed by the future obligation to pay an unknown rent which may be beyond his means. Better to draw a line beyond which his liability must cease and to take his chance under the Landlord and Tenant Act than tie himself down for many future years with numerous rent reviews stretching into an uncertain future.

All this may change again. I write at a time when business sentiment has suddenly moved from pessimism to optimism. The more bullish the economy and the greater the demand for premises the nearer landlords are likely to get to achieving their ideal. This, I would postulate, is the grant of a long lease on full repairing terms with frequent upwards rent reviews and with substantial personal covenants either from the tenants themselves or from their directors offering guarantees. The lower the demand for premises, the more likely it is that landlords have to deviate from such an ideal.

In recent years some specific trends can be identified, but it is precisely the market mechanisms I discussed above which will determine whether or not they become increasingly common.

Clear leases

Take, for instance, the creation of 'clear leases' whereby the landlord of a building in multiple occupation passes all his obligations on to the tenants by way of a service charge. Where there is a substantial demand, landlords have been quite successful in establishing this but in many cases tenants successfully resist the landlord's attempt to impose capital costs upon them. The House of Lords decision in *O'May* v. *City of London Real Property Co.* (1982) was a clear signal that landlords could not introduce terms of this kind when leases were being renewed under the 1954 Act. However, service charges, which were once the preserve of long residential leases, are becoming increasingly common features in commercial lettings. Some statutory intervention in this field equivalent to the service charge provisions of the 1980 Housing Act, seems overdue.

A share in the tenant's gross?

A trend that has not developed to any great extent has been the idea that landlords should participate in the turnover (or perhaps even the profits) of their tenants' enterprises. This is fairly common in the United States, particularly on the development of new shopping precincts. In the UK, however, this seems not to have happened, perhaps because the mechanism of renewal and the allied science of rent review have now become so well established that landlords see the establishment of satisfactory comparables as their best opportunity for enhancing their investments. After all, they are in the property business so why should they tie their rental prospects to those of the clothing factory, hi-fi shop, dance studio or whatever the enterprise of their tenant may be?

Government intervention

Will we ever again see government intervention in the field of commercial rents? The experiment of controlling these in the early 70s was not considered a success. It did not apply to new lettings. Landlords and tenants reviewed or renewed all existing lettings as if the freeze did not exist in the confident expectation that it would shortly end (which of course it did), so that the only consequence was a temporary revenue loss. With institutions such as banks and insurance companies so heavily involved in business property investment, the reintroduction of controls would have wide-reaching consequences for those institutions. The beneficiaries of insurance and pension policies issued by such bodies would also suffer.

The period of business rent control led to severe financial crises. Banks and institutions had lent money in the expectation that their customers would receive an increased rental on review or renewal of their tenants' leases, and property owners had borrowed money in the confident belief that any shortfall between interest payable and rents received would disappear on review. The control of business rents made it difficult or impossible for some investors to service their loans and undermined the security of loans and property values. I suspect that, having burned their fingers once, governments of any complexion are unlikely to try again.

Suggestions for reform

It is therefore most likely that it will be market forces rather than intervention by the government which determines the future shape of business lettings. Within the overall statutory framework of the 1954 Act there are, nevertheless, some reforms which could improve the system.

It seems to me that tenants, whilst having reasonable protection from the 1954 Act, need some further assistance in the case of their long term obligations. It is well recognised that the position of an original lessee and of a guarantor is inequitable and should be changed. An original lessee or someone who has signed a guarantee for the remainder of the term of a lease may find himself pursued by the landlord when he has no further connection with the property. The lease may have changed hands several times. On each occasion the landlord will almost certainly have seen references and given his consent. Over the years, a number of rent reviews may have taken place so the passing rent will be substantially higher than the figure to which the original tenant or guarantor put his signature. Surely the law should intervene to remove these long term liabilities, particularly where the landlord has given his express consent to the lease being taken over by the new tenant? Admittedly, such a reform might result in landlords resisting changes of tenancy where they feel the quality of their covenant is being diminished, and it might be necessary to redraw the definition of 'reasonableness' so that the reform would not create a substantial obstacle for the transfer of tenancies between businessmen. However, I feel quite sure that a shift of the balance is needed.

Statutory regulation of rent reviews?

Another matter in which the state could reasonably intervene is that of rent reviews. There has been an unwarranted amount of litigation on the subject of the timing of review notices, the legitimacy of artificial 'assumptions' written into the lease and so forth. The matter is highly technical and it requires considerable competence and persistence on the part of the tenant's solicitors to resist the imposition of unfair rent review terms. Often, the market forces I discussed above persuade the tenant he must accept such terms even if they are manifestly unfair. A measure of reform which laid down standard assumptions akin to those of the 1954 Act would make the process more predictable without being unduly unfair to the landlord.

It would be sensible to lay down statutory guidelines to govern the limits within which a rent review notice (or the implementation of a rent review procedure) would be valid. Such guidelines would save both landlords and tenants from the consequences of minor delays or oversights while at the same time setting outside time limits beyond which a review would be lost. On the one hand, a degree of human error on the part of the landlords or their advisers would not be fatal even if the lease stated 'time to be of the essence'. On the other, landlords would not be able to take advantage of the recent trend in case law allowing almost indefinite extension of the review times and thus threatening to leave tenants with very substantial arrears to meet once a deferred review is finally settled.

Meanings the Landlord and Tenant Act did not intend

The science of rent review negotiations and the stream of judicial decisions on the subject have created situations which, whatever the meaning the courts may have ascribed to the words they used, the landlords and tenants clearly did not intend. Unless Parliament intervenes, some of these problems will be with us until the leases in question expire – perhaps for ninety-nine years.

It is, surely, inequitable that a tenant should have to pay a reviewed rent on his own improvements unless the lease he signed makes it crystal clear that he agreed to do so. Surely, too, it is wrong for the rent to be inflated as a result of wholly fictitious assumptions in the review clause. For instance, it can not be right that a tenant with a twenty-five year lease with five-yearly reviews should have his rent assessed as if the lease were for a twenty-five year term without review? There are further examples too numerous to mention.

Preserving the tenant's 1954 Act rights

At present, after the landlord has served the tenant with 1954 Act notice the tenant can lose his right to a new tenancy if he fails to serve his counter-notice or apply to the court in time. The recent revision of the statutory forms which now contain prominent warning notices is of some help, but in a situation where the landlord holds most of the cards it should perhaps be less easy for the tenant to lose his rights by default.

What is required is a system which provides predictability and fairness, giving either party who has slipped up every chance to retrieve himself. Even my relatively brief survey of renewal rights under the 1954 Act and of the 1927 Act makes it self-evident that, whatever the virtues of the overall scheme, detailed reforms additions and amendments are now long overdue.

Until such reforms are introduced, it is the duty of solicitors and surveyors to protect their clients and to defend their clients' interests when agreeing the terms of new leases or operating the terms of existing leases. It is the desire of the professional man to be fair minded, but it is his duty to advise his clients and to carry out their instructions.

Tempering market forces

If one has a general belief in the efficacy of market forces in the allocation of resources, then the influence of those forces on the supply of business property must in the long run be beneficial. Having said that, whose responsibility should it be to protect businessmen who are providing a valuable service in the face of the ravages of those market forces? It is the dilemma of the corner shopkeeper who cannot make ends meet but will be sorely missed when he finally closes down. The providers of useful services such as electricians, bicycle repairers and craftsmen of various kinds, cannot hope to meet the substantial rents which can be easily afforded by businesses with a high turnover or greater profit margins. What is the right answer?

Rent control akin to that in the residential sector would distort the market and deprive many legitimate investors of a return on their capital. There are local authorities who take it upon themselves to provide what might be called 'sheltered accommodation' for such small business ventures. Clearly, as old gives way to new in city centres and draughts make way for air conditioning, some way must be found to help the business tenant (and his landlord) to accommodate some of society's genuine needs.

Appendix A

Specimen letter of instructions

Messrs Black White & Co
Solicitors
Lloyds Bank Chambers
High Street
Camford OX3 2RJ

Dear Sirs

re: 1st floor offices, 19 Regent Street, Camford

Subject to contract

We have pleasure in setting out below details of the letting we have negotiated on behalf of our mutual clients Town Centre Offices Limited. We trust these will enable you to submit a draft lease as soon as possible to the prospective tenants' solicitors.

1. Premises

The office suite on the first floor of the building. We enclose three copies of a floor plan showing the extent of the demise edged in red. The tenants will have the right to use the passenger lift and the ladies and gentlemen's toilets which are situated between the ground and first floors.

2. Tenants

The tenants are Forward Publicity Limited. Their registered office is at 22 New Quebec Street London W1. Their solicitors are Messrs. Brown Green & Co. of 25 High Street, Oxbridge CA3 4PD (for the attention of Mr Grey).

3. Guarantors

Mr Philip Forward and Mrs Joan Robinson who are directors of the company will offer their personal guarantees.

4. Term

Fifteen years from 29th September this year.

5. Rent

The initial rent is £16,000 per annum but the tenants will be allowed an initial rent free period of three months during which they will be expected to redecorate the interior of the property. The rent will be subject to upwards only reviews at the end of each fifth year of the term.

6. Repairs

The tenants will be required to keep the interior of the property in good repair and to contribute to the cost of external decoration and structural repairs through our mutual clients' service charge scheme.

7. Permitted Use

The tenants will wish to use the premises as offices for their advertising business. The lease should, however, simply permit general use as offices.

8. Alterations

Our mutual clients have agreed the tenants may erect non structural partitions so long as they undertake to remove these and make good at the end of the term.

9. Subletting

Our mutual clients are most concerned that the first floor should not be further subdivided so please ensure that a suitable restriction is inserted in the lease to that effect.

10. Timing

The premises are vacant now. As we have approved the tenants references and in view of the rent free period, our clients are anxious to conclude the formalities as quickly as possible. If necessary please arrange for the tenants to be allowed into occupation under licence or for a suitable agreement for lease to be signed if this will save time.

11. Costs

The tenants have agreed to meet your proper charges
in connection with the preparation of the lease.

We trust the above provides you with sufficient
information but please do not hesitate to contact us if
any further details are required.

Yours faithfully,

Appendix B

Checklist for tenants

HEADING	D E T A I L S	NOTE
HEAD/UNDERLEASE	Dated........../New..Yes...	
PREMISES	1st Floor, 19 Regent Street CAMFORD Rights included..Lift: WCs......... (goods×lift/parking/loading×etc) Rights excluded... No weekend use	
TERM	...15...years from..29 Sept 19 85 expires....28 Sept 19 2000 early termination? No	
PARTIES	Landlord..Town Centre Offices Ltd, tenant.....Forward Publicity Ltd guarantors.P Forward & Mrs J Robinson	
RENT:	.£16,000........... p.a. exclusive/inclusive×of rates rent free period..3 months.. payable in advance/arrears:× usual quarter days/ yes interest 5%..over Base after 14..days	

REVIEW:	after ...5th & 10th.......years:
	next review... 29 Sept 1990
	notice needed..No...........
	Assume: VP. Full/Residue of term
	        actual/deemed use
	        other........good repair.
	Disregard: Goodwill×Occupation×
	           Improvements
	           Other.... No
		Amend to
		include

REPAIR by Tenant	EXT.. No .. Decorate every.-...yrs INT.. Yes. Decorate every..5..yrs Yes party/shared structures.......... Tenant to meet s.146 Costs.. Yes..	
SERVICE CHARGE	Estimated per annum:£.. Not stated Services provided (see below) Includes:Installations?..Renewal? Reserve fund?... No............	Ask for details

CAN TENANT (with Consent)
(*='Not to be unreasonably withheld')

DEALINGS	Assign whole..Yes.*.Assign part..No... Sublet whole..Yes.*Sublet part..No..
ALTERATIONS	Alter ext/structure No alter int...Yes...Shopfront..N/A..
USE	Change use....Yes.* for other office use Specified use.office.for.advert Prohibited use(s).No.res..use
STATUTES	The tenant must obey Planning Acts...Yes.............. Other Statutes...Yes..............
OTHER TENANT'S COVENANTS	Only authorised nameplate allowed ....
LANDLORDS COVENANTS	Quiet Enjoyment..Yes.. Observe Headlease..N/A.. Repair...Yes.(so long as service charge paid) Provide services (see below) Yes (as above) other.....No................. Insure....Yes..............
INSURANCE	By Landlord/Tenant At expense of Landlord/Tenant Normal risks.OK.Property Owners.OK. Years loss of rent insured..3..... Years rent suspended....3......
1954 ACT	Renewal rights excluded?..No...... Compensation excluded?....Yes... (ineffective after 5 years)
FORFEITURE	If rent unpaid for......14....days For insolvency....Yes..........
SURETY CLAUSE	Surety bound till tenancy ends..? Yes till lease assigned? No Surety to take lease in own name? Yes
OTHER PROVISIONS	T. to pay legal costs .... .Note.restrictive.hours.(no.weekend use) Amend!

SERVICE CHARGE SCHEDULE
(Items Landlord may provide and charge to tenants)

Exterior painting/Structure	Yes	
Central Heating/Hot water	Yes	
Lift maintenance/renewal	Yes	Try & Delete
Clean/light common parts	Yes	'renewal'
Staff	No	
Other	Entryphone. Refuse disposal Management fees (15%) Sprinkler system	Does building have Fire Certificate?

Table of Cases

The following abbreviations of Reports are used:

Table of statutes

Index